I0108656

A Virtuous Woman:

The Fairytale Story

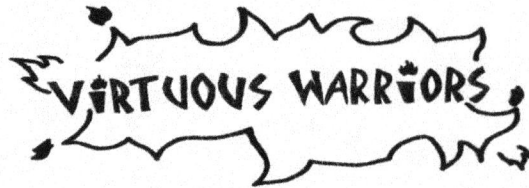

Other Bible Studies in the Virtuous Warriors Series

By Sharon Hoskins

Rebekah's Confidence

The F.E.A.R. of the Lord

A Virtuous Woman: The Fairytale Story

By

Sharon Hoskins

Proverbs 31:30 Ministry

2014

Copyright © 2014 by Sharon Hoskins

All rights reserved. This book or any portion thereof may not be reproduced or used in any manner whatsoever without the express written permission of the publisher except for the use of brief quotations in a book review or scholarly journal.

All Scripture quotations, unless otherwise indicated, are taken from The Holy Bible, New King James Version, copyright 1982 by Thomas Nelson, Inc.

Definitions, unless otherwise indicated are taken from Merriam Webster Online

ISBN: 978-0-9908245-1-0

Edited by Shayla Soehrmann

Virtuous Warriors design by Kristi Johnson
Cover picture is Gloria Spencer and Jamie Lincoln
Back cover picture is Jamie Lincoln

Contents

Preface

A Virtuous Woman began as a short study written for a ladies retreat. I hosted this retreat a couple of times for different churches and used it as an outline that took me from the original four chapters to the fifteen chapters found in this study. When I first started to write, I didn't know how much this study would impact my own life. In the beginning chapters, God reminded me of my journey as a new Christian, and impressed upon me to share those testimonies. But, it was Chapter Nine before I realized how personal this book had become. I was stuck on this chapter for over a year. The title began as "open communication" and instantly I knew that this was for me. My husband and I were having a very hard time communicating and I thought, "If he doesn't change, I will never get past this chapter!" Oh, how good I was at pointing my finger to his problem. I prayed for him and begged God to show him his faults. I wanted so desperately to finish this book before the end of 2012 and began to think God was never going to answer my prayer.

A little over a year later, God spoke to me about my own heart, and revealed all the fingers of disrespect and unforgiveness pointing back at me. God did a miracle in my life and changed the title to "respect." As a Christian, I have learned to be very transparent and share testimonies about what God has taught me, but this testimony was so difficult to give because I started sharing it immediately. It is easier to share a testimony when it's a couple of months or years old, but when it just happened, it is humiliating. However, this has been such a rewarding testimony because it has touched so many lives as I share.

Through this book, I have learned a lot about myself. I told my dear friend, Gloria Spencer, that by the time I finished this book; maybe I would be a virtuous woman. Gloria is the kind of friend that will tell me the truth, no matter how hard it is. Early in my Christian walk, her words of correction put me back on the right track when she told me during a pity party that I just needed to get right with God. My jaw dropped and I gasped in shock, but as I considered her words and prayed, I realized she was right. She says she doesn't even remember saying that but she changed my life that day, and I learned how to have a proper pity party that got me through some tough times. She plays the part of Naomi on the front cover.

I am thankful for the Christian friends God has put in my life. They have helped me through difficulties with prayer, truth, and love. I am so thankful to God for giving me the courage to share my mistakes and failures. It is humiliating, but at the same time, it is so rewarding. I am thankful that God gave me a husband who endured with his wife in love, even when I was unlovable. I am thankful for the story of Ruth and Naomi, who were a testimony that changed my life. I truly pray

The Fairytale Story

that this book will impact your lives as much as it has mine. As you study, be willing to look deep in your heart and repent, don't get stuck as I did, the sooner you look at yourselves the better you will grow. Take every opportunity to share with others what God has taught you. Never be ashamed to share, even if it is humiliating, because the rewards are so much greater. I pray you finish this study successfully finding yourself a virtuous woman in the end.

7

Introduction

A Virtuous Woman is a study of the Book of Ruth. Each chapter of this study focuses on a section of Scripture in Ruth. You can read the Scriptures from your own Bible or read what is provided for you from the NKJV. You will be required to have a Bible to read and answer question throughout the chapters. With any Bible Study, we should find ourselves studying the Bible and applying it to our lives. The purpose of this study is to help us become more virtuous in our everyday living as Christian women. It is important for God to be glorified in our lives and for the characteristics of Christ to be evident in our actions and attitude. This Bible study takes a look at all the people surrounding Ruth and defines how they made a difference in her life. We will discuss how Ruth responds to these people, and how her life parallels to our lives today.

Truly, the love that Ruth and Naomi displayed to each other was God's love. When they arrived in Bethlehem they were poor, alone, and probably felt like life had dealt them a bad hand. However, in the end, life was very good, not because of what anyone did except God through the life of this foreign woman. Our society today looks at our fame, class, wealth, and position to determine if they want to know us. Few look to see the qualities that are within, so we tend to overlook them too. Many times, we are focused on what it takes to "make it in this world," and society tells us what that is. This idea has even spilled over into the church. We decide who can do what in church based on these same set of standards. We have clicks in our churches where a woman who has a beautiful heart is overlooked because she doesn't wear the finest clothes. We don't want to hang out with a woman who has integrity because she doesn't fit our class. We want to be with the beautiful, well-to-do, charming women. They become our role model so we will act like them to be accepted and then we become dissatisfied with our life because we are never able to attain the beauty, charm, or income in comparison.

It is important that we learn to look at women like Ruth as a role model. There is no mention of her beauty or charm and we know she is not wealthy. The beauty of her heart causes her to be desirable and this kind of beauty is attainable only through Jesus. This beauty is something no one can take away, it comes with favor, peace, and joy, and it shines from the inside out. At one time in Ruth's life, she was a woman of the world, a pagan worshiper, until she met God through Naomi. Too many times, we forget that we were once a woman of the world, a sinner, until we met God. Just as Ruth went through the process of change to become virtuous, so must we, regardless of what we look like on the outside. Ruth was willing to make many changes in her life that created beautiful qualities in her heart and because of

Ruth's willingness to change; she helped change the lives of those around her. She continues to help change the lives of women today as we read her story and understand what it means to be a virtuous woman. What could we do in the lives of those around us if we would be virtuous in the sight of all the people in our town? Through this study, we will learn what it means to be like Ruth, a virtuous woman.

Chapter 1: The Fairytale

Once upon a time, there lived a beautiful princess, in a kingdom far, far away. She had golden locks of hair that flowed down her back, her eyes were as clear as the crystal blue sea, and her beauty was natural from birth. She was the most beautiful young lady in all the land, none could compare. She was the dream of every prince in the region and the race was on to see who would be the first to slay the dragon and win her hand in marriage. Every available Prince went to battle with sword and shield. The dragon had his own weapons of fiery flames from his mouth and large tail of defense. As each prince took his turn, the dragon was able to pick him off one by one. Prince John and Prince Edward were the last two to contend, they attacked on each side. A jab at the dragon's leg caused injury but nothing seemed to get it down. In the fight, Prince John lost his shield and the fiery dragon shot out flames, unfortunately, Prince John was taken out of the battle. Prince Edward was the only one left but he still had to slay the dragon. Realizing that he could get the dragon while the attention was on Prince John, Prince Edward climbed his tail, crossed his back, and jabbed his sword right into the head of the enormous beast! The dragon was slain and Prince Edward had won the beautiful princess. After his victory dance he made his way to her, bowed himself, and asked her hand in marriage. Their wedding the next day was the finest in the land. Her gown was adorned with lace and beads. Her bouquet of pink flowers, babies breathe, and greens flowed down from her hands. The wedding cake was ten tiers connected by tiny bridges and running fountains. People from all over came to enjoy this glorious event. It was a ball to remember, everything from the bride to the music was perfect. Now, the "I dos" are said, the cake is cut, the dance is made and the day is done. This is the part where we hear, "and they lived happily ever after."

This is the fairytale we have heard all of our lives, it's the one we hope for, the one we daydream about as little girls, and the one we look for when we begin to date. We want prince charming to come rescue us, sweep us off our feet, and live happily ever after. But the truth to the whole fairytale is that Prince Edward got his Princess and now life begins. They don't really know each other, they don't know how to communicate, and their attraction is only skin-deep. The beauty they see in each other will not be able to hold the marriage together. Prince Edward must love her as Christ loved the church, that he would give his life for her, dying to his wants and desires for hers. The beautiful princess must submit to and respect him, giving him a place of honor in her life, dying to her wants and desires for his.

Now, I'm not going to tell you that the fairytale never happens because I think it does. We all have a romantic story of how we met our special someone, how they swept us off our feet or rescued us from some dragon in our life, but we have so much of the fairytale concept influencing us from everywhere that we can get lost trying to play out our own life in fairy land. At the movies, the guy always gets the girl and they live happily ever after. On television, the series keeps us coming back to see if the guy gets the girl to live happily ever after. In the novels, we find the guy getting the girl in the end to live happily ever after. This idea can get us in trouble when our own real life fairytale comes to the happily ever after. In all the fairytales, I have ever heard, none has ever told of the times you disagree, the times you argue, the times of misunderstandings and miscommunications. The "happily ever after" is only if we decide to see those times through. Marriage does not come easy, it's work, it takes commitment to endure, and it should be forever. I know that many have divorced and this is not a "shame on you" study. As a whole, women have let the fairytales of this world be our guideline for choosing and keeping our mates. We choose them based on their ability to play the fairytale prince. Then, we keep them based on their ability to continue playing that fairytale prince. When they fail, we are disappointed, and when they continue to disappoint, a failed marriage is around the corner. We will then start looking for another prince who will make us feel like a princess, and the process starts all over again. We have done this because we didn't realize that the harmless stories of the "happily ever after" had become not so harmless to our hearts.

These fairytale stories are romantic and most women love romance. We think if we wait for God to put it together that it won't be romantic, but God is not oblivious to romance. He created it and He knows that we like it. Romance makes us feel important and special. It makes us feel as if someone cares enough to make plans with us, to spend time with us, and do things just for us. There is probably not a woman on this planet that doesn't like to be romanced. We all like to know that we are special to someone. We all have a need to be needed, and we all want to feel important. God knows that we have these feelings because He created us with them, but the romance of our lives can be greater than the fairytales of the world if we will allow God to orchestrate it. Even in our marriages, God can create romance when we keep Him in our focus. We know that God has experience in this area because He has been putting men and women together for many, many years.

So, let's stop for a moment and think about the romantic stories orchestrated by God that we find in the Bible. First, we have Adam and Eve. God said, *"It is not good that man should be alone; I will make him an help meet for him"* (KJV). The word "help meet" comes from the root word "succor" which means to give assistance or aid to, to protect and surround, assistance and support in times of hardship and distress. Aid, care for, comfort, support, bring relief to, take care of, look after, and attend to, are synonyms for the word succor. So, God set out to find the perfect helper for him (verse 19). He formed every beast of the field and every bird of the air but there was not found a "help meet or succor" for him (verse 20). God could see that it was not good for Adam to be alone, so God caused a deep sleep to fall upon Adam, and He took one of his ribs. The word rib actually means side, and He made a woman. God gave Adam the perfect "help meet or succor", she was the one created just for him, and they were perfectly matched because God did it.

I am sure there was plenty of romance that sparked between them. They were perfect together and even though they completed each other, they were already complete within themselves. Eve did not need Adam to make her a complete person, just as Adam did not need Eve to be a complete person. She had characteristics that made her who she was, and Adam did too. She had a personality all her own and her actions reflected her heart, just as Adam's did. None of these things about her depended on Adam, but together they were complete *for* each other, not *with* each other. When we add one and one it makes two, but just as we have learned in math class, if either of these is not a whole, then they are a fraction. So, we must be whole within ourselves to be perfectly joined to the one we are with, or going to be with. If we are not whole then we try to take from the other to build our wholeness. This doesn't work because we are all individuals and uniquely made. We need to find our own wholeness in the Lord and not rely on others to fill us up, only God can fill the places that are lacking within. God created Eve whole, and He created Adam whole; and the two became one; husband and wife. There is great honor and a sense of fulfillment in being a wife and Eve got to be the first one. There is something beautiful about being that woman. A wife that is dependable, trustworthy, encouraging, and loving that he is proud to have you walk beside him and you are proud to be there.

God's purpose for creating women was not to put them in a place of servitude. It was not to be barefoot and pregnant in the kitchen. We have fought so hard against these degrading positions that we have gone overboard. We want things to be all our way and we will not give up our wants for any man, unless of course, we are trying to catch him. We will be whatever a guy wants us to be and do whatever he wants us to do until we catch him, and marry him, then we want to stand up for our rights. I have seen this many times in our young ladies over the years. I have seen it with women who have been in abusive relationships in their past. It seems to be some instinctive defense mechanism for their heart. However, God did not create us to compete with each other. If we look at the definition of compete, *it is to strive consciously or unconsciously for an objective (as position, profit, or a prize), to be in a state of rivalry*. God did not intend for us to be in a fight for rights or positions but that's what marriage and relationships have become. It's as if we want our knight and shining armor to come rescue us only so we can knock him down, strip him of his shield, and make him our slave. It's as though we have the need to get it done to him before he does it to us. This is unfair, not only to the guy being caught, but also to ourselves. If we are being whatever a guy wants because we are afraid he won't like us, then insecurity has a rule on our life. We are not being true to who we are and the guy is not getting to know the real person, so the marriage, if it comes to that, is based on a fictitious character, but the truth comes out eventually in the battle for rights. We do this because we are not whole and complete. The definition of complete, *it is filled up; with no part or element lacking; free from deficiency; entire; perfect; consummate.* Being complete will cause us to be confident and sure of whom we are. We will know what we believe in. We will have a standard that we are true to and live by.

So, how do we know if we are whole, confident, sure, and complete within ourselves? Start by asking yourself these questions.

1. Am I easily influenced to go along with what someone else believes or do I stand on what I know to be true in my heart? _____

_____

_____

_____

_____

2. Am I able to make a decision based on what I know to be true in my heart or do I need someone else to help me decide? _____

_____

_____

_____

_____

3. Based on the situation and the person I am with, do I change what I believe or do I really know what I believe in my heart. _____

_____

_____

_____

_____

It is so important that we know ourselves so we can confidently be ourselves around that special someone. Many times, we hide who we really are because we are afraid that we won't be liked or that we will be ridiculed for what we believe. It's important to be true to ourselves and not compromise for others just to win approval. When we compromise and win approval of others, then we only cheat ourselves but when we are confident and whole, the result will be a fulfillment of love for ourselves. This love gives us confidence in whom we are and what we believe in, then a realness that comes from the depths of our soul will be shown, and we will receive real love in return when we give it. How can we ask someone else to love us if we don't love ourselves?

We will be better wives, mothers, daughters, and friends when we are confident, sure, and complete within ourselves. We will then look more like the Proverbs 31 Woman who was a Virtuous Woman. The word virtue has been defined as *reserved, stiff, and over-sensitive* but these are definitions connected to the word prude. Women do not want to be labeled as a prude and they don't want to be around women who are prudes so they have rejected the idea of being virtuous because they haven't understood the meaning. If we look at the true meaning of virtue, it is *moral excellence, merit, good quality, female chastity, power, or efficacy*. Virtuous means *upright, dutiful, and chaste (pure and simple in taste and style)*. Most women want these words used when others describe them. Unfortunately, we have ran from being virtuous, either because we thought we could never attain it or because we didn't want to be stiff and over-sensitive. Now that we know what it means to be virtuous, and to have virtue in the fruit of our life, as we go through this study, remember, every time we say virtue it means moral excellence, and every time we say virtuous it means upright and chaste.

Read 2 Peter 1:5-11 and answer the questions below.

1. What is the first thing that we should add to our faith? _____

Our faith is when we come into a relationship with God the Father through His Son, Jesus, and then we start a journey by allowing God to change us from bad qualities to good ones. These changes are a process that creates a new person inside.

2. What should we add to our virtue? _____

As we become more virtuous, then the knowledge of God will grow, because we are not rejecting the knowledge based on our immoral lives. It is hard for us to accept the knowledge that God says to love if we hate, or to have compassion if we have anger, and to be sexually pure if we are sexually immoral. Resisting virtue will keep us from growing in the grace and knowledge of our Lord and Savior Jesus Christ. (2 Peter 3:18)

3. What are the next two things that we should add? _____
_____

As we obtain knowledge of who God is, and what He expects, then we must have self-control and perseverance to allow changes in our life. Self-control is needed to discipline our own actions and attitude to be more like Christ. Perseverance is needed to continue to discipline ourselves.

4. What does verse 6 say to add to perseverance? _____

As we add self-control and perseverance to our life, when we have obtained knowledge, then we become more like Christ in godliness.

5. What next two things should then be added? _____

How can we be godly without first adding virtue and knowledge? How can we show God's love without first having patience and self-control? This growing process will help us never stumble and enter abundantly into the everlasting kingdom of our Lord and Savior Jesus Christ. (2 Peter 1:10-11)

Virtue is part of our first steps in Christianity, without it, we can add nothing to our faith. God has given examples in the Bible of virtuous women for us to learn from and admire. Many women like Rebekah, Esther, and Mary who showed virtue in the fruit of their life as they obeyed God against all adversity. Our example in this study is Ruth. Not only is she described as being virtuous, but she also allowed God to orchestrate a romantic story of her life. She is the princess who is rescued by a prince, not because she was royalty, or because she was beautiful, but because she was virtuous. *"...for all the people of my town know that you are a virtuous woman."* Ruth 3:11 Now that we know a little more about ourselves and understand what it means to be virtuous, let's examine our own lives, as we look at the evidence of Ruth, and strive to be a virtuous woman.

Chapter 2: Set the Stage

Ruth 1:1-7

₁Now it came to pass, in the days when the judges ruled, that there was a famine in the land. And a certain man of Bethlehem, Judah, went to dwell in the country of Moab, he and his wife and his two sons. ₂The name of the man was Elimelech, the name of his wife was Naomi, and the names of his two sons were Mahlon, and Chilion – Ephrathites of Bethlehem, Judah. And they went to the country of Moab and remained there. ₃Then Elimelech, Naomi's husband, died; and she was left, and her two sons. ₄Now they took wives of the women of Moab; the name of the one was Orpah, and the name of the other Ruth. And they dwelt there about ten years. ₅Then both Mahlon and Chilion also died; so the woman survived her two sons and her husband. ₆Then she arose with her daughters-in-law that she might return from the country of Moab, for she had heard in the country of Moab that the Lord had visited His people in giving them bread. ₇Therefore she went out from the place where she was, and her two daughters-in-law with her; and they went on the way to return to the land of Judah.

These verses set the stage for us to understand what happens to cause this family to reside in the land of Moab. A famine had struck Judah, so to keep his family alive Elimelech moves them to Moab. He does not have enough faith to stay in Bethlehem to allow God to provide for him. It looks as though fear causes him to make a decision outside of faith. In the process of this decision, he sets the stage for his children to take foreign wives and for his wife to be a widow in a foreign land. His decision also affects Ruth and Orpah. It is amazing how much our decisions affect others in our lives, and when we make decisions out of fear, we will quickly find ourselves out of God's plan. It is natural, in the decision making process, to look at how it will benefit our life, and we are oblivious to what it will do to someone else. Each one of us can look back at our past and see how the decisions that others made set the stage for a course in our life. These decisions could be a move, as it was for Naomi, or it could be a job, divorce, adoption, addiction, or any number of other things. However big or small, the decision affects our lives, whether good or bad. It is especially important for parents to remember that the decisions we make will set the stage for our children, just as it did for Mahlon and Chilion. However, it is not restricted to the children, but it also affects others around us. Our faith is seen in the decisions we make. Naomi's life is affected by the fearful decision to move to Moab. Now, she has to make a decision, which will set the stage for another chapter in her life, and the lives of her daughters-in-law. When she hears that the famine is over in Judah she has nothing left to keep her in Moab, and decides to return home to Bethlehem. This decision requires very little faith, because she has already heard that the famine is over, but she hopes to find comfort from her extended family, the familiarity of a lifestyle, and friends that she left behind.

Naomi finds herself in a situation that she has no control over, but she musters up what little faith she has left in her to make a decision that puts her back in God's plan. I'm sure we all find ourselves in situations that we have no control over, and must muster every bit of faith within us to get through it. If we have strong, mature Christians in our life, we can seek wisdom and prayers, but to see things through it will take faith. How we handle ourselves in situations will set the stage for those around us to see our faith and possibly come to know our God, so it is very important in Christianity to walk by faith and not by sight. *"But without faith it is impossible to please Him, for he who comes to God must believe that He is, and that He is a rewarder of those who diligently seek Him."*

Pray and ask God to show you what you can change in your life to set a better stage for those around you? _____
_____
_____
_____

Who in the Bible set the stage for all people to live by? _____

The biggest stage is set by Jesus. In all that Jesus does, from the beginning of His life to the death of the cross, He set the stage for a new way of life for all of us. Through His obedience, we can receive the promise of the Holy Spirit. *"Nevertheless I tell you the truth. It is to your advantage that I go away; for if I do not go away, the Helper will not come to you; but if I depart, I will send Him to you."* John 16:7. The role of the Holy Spirit is vital for a relationship with God. *"In Him (Christ) you also trusted, after you heard the word of truth, the gospel of your salvation; in whom also, having believed, you were sealed with the Holy Spirit of promise."* Ephesians 1:13. The meanings of the word believe are to trust in, cling to, rely upon, and commit unto. This is for each individual person who receives the word of truth, the good news of their salvation in a relationship with God the Father through His Son, Jesus, as they cling to Him, rely upon Him, trust Him, and commit their lives to Him. Through that belief, we receive the Holy Spirit to help us live as Christ, which we must do by faith.

Read John 14:15-26 and answer the questions below.

1. What does verse 16 say about the Holy Spirit (Helper or Comforter)? _____
_____
_____

2. Why can the world not receive the Holy Spirit (Spirit of truth), according to verse 17? _____
_____

3. So, what must we do to receive the Holy Spirit? _____
_____
_____

4. What does verse 26 say the Holy Spirit will do for us? _____
_____
_____

5. So, what must we do for the Holy Spirit to bring to our remembrance what Jesus said? _____
_____

The Holy Spirit is given to us when we come into a relationship with the Father through Jesus, His Son, by faith. In this relationship, we will read the Bible, and the Holy Spirit will bring to our remembrance what His word says. We will get to know Him through His word, and begin to see Him and hear Him as He speaks to us through the Holy Spirit. We will pray and diligently seek Him, and God will speak to us through the Holy Spirit. We will listen to our pastors and teachers to gain knowledge of God and His ways. As we grow to know Him more, we will love Him more, obey Him more, and we will set the stage for others to come to know Him also.

Read John 14:27-31 and answer the questions below.

1. What does Jesus say about our heart in verse 27? _____
_____

2. Write verse 31. _____

3. Who does Jesus want to know that He loves the Father? _____

4. How does Jesus show His love to the Father? _____
_____

Jesus didn't question the Father, He didn't have to understand why; He just did what the Father commanded. Being filled with the Holy Spirit will guide us in all truth and strengthen our faith to follow God's plan even when we don't understand it. Elimelech's fear over a famine leads his family out of God's plan. He let fear replace his faith in the one true God to provide and protect them. We can allow fear to creep in our heart a little at a time. We may not even think that it is fear, just as Elimelech probably didn't think that he moved in fear.

When my first child was getting old enough to go to public school, I was so scared that she would be hurt or ridiculed that I couldn't bring myself to let her go. I already had her in a private school a couple of days a week, so I begged my husband to allow her to stay there one more year, then one more year, then one more year, until the end of her first grade. When I finally gave in and allowed her to go to public school, she was so far behind state and federal standards that she had to be held back and repeat her first grade again. I let my fear keep me from making the right decision and set the stage for her to repeat a year of school. Now, I'm not trying to say good or bad about one school or another, but that it was fear that made my decision. All of us can probably look at our lives and find somewhere that we have allowed fear to make decisions for us, but we don't have to continue to allow that to happen anymore. We can learn from our mistakes and the mistake that we can see Elimelech make, by allowing the Holy Spirit to guide us in all truth and replace our fear with faith. As we walk by faith, we will set the stage for others to walk by faith also. We should be obedient to God, live to righteousness, and practice such things that glorify the Father, just as Jesus did, so that others will be encouraged to do the same, and set a stage for Christ in their life.

Pray and ask God to show you if you are allowing fear to make decisions for you, ask Him to help strengthen your faith and trust in Him. *"For God has not given us a spirit of fear, but of power and of love and of a sound mind."* 2 Timothy1:7. Then ask Him to show you how you can make better decisions that will set a better stage for others to find Jesus. Write down the answer God gives you. _____
_____
_____

_____

Chapter 3: Set an Example

Ruth 1:8-13

8And Naomi said to her two daughters-in-law, "Go, return each to her mother's house. The Lord deal kindly with you, as you have dealt with the dead and with me. 9The Lord grant that you may find rest, each in the house of her husband." So she kissed them, and they lifted up their voices and wept. 10And they said to her, "Surely we will return with you to your people." 11But Naomi said, "Turn back, my daughters; why will you go with me? Are there still sons in my womb, that they may be your husbands? 12Turn back, my daughters, go---for I am too old to have a husband. If I should say I have hope, even if I should have a husband tonight and should also bear sons, 13would you wait for them till they were grown? Would you restrain yourselves from having husbands? No, my daughters; for it grieves me very much for your sakes that the hand of the Lord has gone out against me!"

Naomi was setting an example, before her daughters-in-law, of the kind of woman she was and the God she served. As she traveled, she realized that she was taking these two women from the only home they had ever known and from their entire family. Naomi urged them to turn back. She knew what it felt like to live in a foreign land, away from all she had ever known; besides she had nothing more to offer them. She loved them both so much that it broke her heart to see them go, but she knew that it was the right thing to do for them. When Naomi realized she was being selfish then she corrected it because of love. *"Love suffers long and is kind; love does not envy; love does not parade itself, is not puffed up; does not behave rudely, does not seek its own, is not provoked, thinks no evil; does not rejoice in iniquity, but rejoices in truth; bears all things, believes all things, hopes all things, endures all things."* 1 Corinthians 13:4-7. Love is the evidence of a Christian in a relationship with God. *"God is love, and he who abides in love abides in God, and God in him."* 1 John 4:16. Naomi set an example of a Christian, because of her love, and *"love never fails."* 1 Corinthians 13:8. She made some mistakes in her grief, but was not too prideful to admit she was wrong, and then she took the steps to make it right. This act of love showed Ruth and Orpah that she cared more for their well-being, than she did her own. When we know God, then we will glorify Him and set an example of love to others in our life.

1. What does Naomi do in verses 8 and 9 that showed her faith in God? _____

_____

_____

_____

_____

2. In what ways can you show your faith in God through prayer? _____

_____

_____

_____

_____

3. What kind of example are you being to those around you? _____

_____

_____

_____

_____

4. What things could you change to set a better example of a Christian? _____

_____

_____

_____

_____

5. Who in the Bible set an example for all people to live by? _____

Jesus was the greatest example of love. *"This is My commandment, that you love one another as I have loved you. Greater love has no one than this, than to lay down one's life for his friends."* John 14:12-13. *"By this we know love, because He (Jesus) laid down His life for us. And we also ought to lay down our lives for the brethren"* 1 John 3:16 Jesus said that the greatest commandment is love to God. *"You shall love the Lord your God with all your heart, with all your soul, and with all your mind. This is the first and great commandment."* Matthew 22:37-38. It seems that true love has been taken out of our definition of Christianity. We have defined love to God as church attendance, charitable deeds, and monetary donations. Many times, I hear people talk about their church attendance, how much money they give, and all their good deeds. A guy told me once that he hasn't missed Sunday church in 30 years. I was surprised! I didn't even know he was a Christian. As I examined his life over the past few years I had known him, I couldn't see a commitment to Christ at all. He looked like a lost man to me from the things he did to the jokes he told, but apparently, he was committed to church attendance. I have heard people talk about how they did good deeds for their neighbor, and how good it made them feel. Others have shared how much money they have given, hoping to attain a position or some special favor. If we research Scripture, we will find that the definition of love to God is obedience. If we tell God we love Him, and we do all these deeds to prove our love, but have no obedience to Him, then where is our love? The obedience He is looking for is not what we can do with our hands, but what we do with our heart.

Read Romans 12:1-21 and answer the questions below.

1. What is our reasonable service? _____

_____

2. What proves that good, acceptable, and perfect will of God? _____

_____

3. What instruction do we have in verse 3 about how we think? _____

_____

_____

4. What understandings are we given about the body of Christ in verses 4-5? ____

_____

_____

5. What does verse 6-8 say about our differing gifts? _____

_____

_____

6. What does verse 9 instruct us to do? _____

_____

_____

7. What does verse 10 say that we should do? _____

_____

_____

8. How are we to serve the Lord, according to verse 11? _____

_____

9. What are the three principles given in verse 12? _____

_____

10. How are we to treat the saints, according to verse 13? _____

_____

_____

11. How are we to treat those who persecute us? _____

_____

_____

12. What kind of heart do we see in verse 15? _____

_____

_____

13. How are we to conduct ourselves according to verse 16? _____

_____

_____

14. What testimony are we to have according to verses 17-18? _____

_____

_____

15. What is our instruction for vengeance in verse 19? _____

_____

_____

16. How are we to treat our enemies according to verse 20? _____

_____

_____

17. How are we to overcome evil according to verse 21? _____

_____

_____

18. In reading through these scriptures, which part convicted your heart? _____

_____

_____

_____

_____

This is how we check our heart; when reading the Bible, or hearing a message of truth, if we feel embarrassed or ashamed that we do not measure up to the commands, then we know God is speaking to us about that particular thing. So, the answers that you wrote on question 18 are things that you personally need to repent of and ask God to forgive you for, and then practice doing what His word says. God will forgive you and it is important that we also forgive others and ourselves.

When we look deep in our heart and examine ourselves, then we can draw closer to the Lord each day. *"Examine yourselves as to whether you are in the faith. Prove yourselves. Do you not know yourselves, that Jesus Christ is in you? – unless indeed you are disqualified"* 2 Cor. 13:5. *"For if we would judge ourselves, we would not be judged"* 1 Cor. 11:31. It is difficult to ask God to show us our hearts because we are afraid of what He may show us. There is no shame and nothing to be afraid of, God loves us and when we love Him, we want to know so we can draw closer to Him. *"He who has My commandments and keeps them, it is he who loves Me. And he who loves Me will be loved by My Father, and I will love him and manifest Myself to him."* John 14:21. *"If anyone loves Me, he will keep My word; and My Father will love him, and We will come to him and make Our home with him."* John 14:23. Romans chapter 12 gives us an understanding of our responsibility toward God, the saints, and our enemies. If we will examine ourselves, and walk in the responsibility of our relationship, we will set an example of what Christianity looks like to others around us.

There are many people trying to get to heaven by doing good deeds, going to church, and giving of their abundance, but none of these things will get them to heaven. *"Most assuredly, I say to you, unless one is born of water and the Spirit, he cannot enter the kingdom of God. That which is born of the flesh is flesh, and that which is born of the Spirit is spirit."* John 3:5-6. *"Whoever has been born of God does not sin, for His seed remains in him; and he cannot sin, because he has been born of God. In this the children of God and the children of the devil are manifest: Whoever does not practice righteousness is not of God, nor is he who does not love his brother."* 1 John 3:9-10.

This should open our eyes to see that we can't live like the devil and still go to heaven. *"Therefore I will judge you, O house of Israel, every one according to his ways, says the Lord God. Repent, and turn from all your transgressions, so that iniquity will not be your ruin. Cast away from you all the transgressions which you have committed, and get yourselves a new heart and a new spirit. For why should you die, O house of Israel? For I have no pleasure in the death of one who dies, says the Lord God. Therefore turn and live!"* Ezekiel 18:30-32. The choice is ours; God will judge us according to our ways. Maybe we need to get a new heart and a new spirit. If that is you today, don't hesitate, repent, turn, and live, then set an example so others may live also.

Jesus set an example of love to His Father before the disciples. He tells the disciples, after washing their feet, *"For I have given you an example, that you should do as I have done to you."* John 13:15. However, we don't see in Scripture that the disciples washed anyone's feet, but we do see them preaching the gospel. They shared truth about how to have a relationship with the Father. They preached repentance, obedience, and love. Jesus said, *"If you keep My commandments, you will abide in My love, just as I have kept My Father's commandments and abide in His love."* John 15:10. Through a lifestyle of prayer and obedience, Jesus set an example for the disciples to have a relationship with the Father and they set an example for others to have a relationship with the Father. Now, it is our turn, as Christians, to set an example for those around us to have a relationship with the Father.

Chapter 4: Change

Ruth 1:14-18

14Then they lifted up their voices and wept again; and Orpah kissed her mother-in-law, but Ruth clung to her. 15And she said, "Look, your sister-in-law has gone back to her people and to her gods; return after your sister-in-law." 16But Ruth said: "Entreat me not to leave you or to turn back from following after you; for wherever you go, I will go; and wherever you lodge, I will lodge; your people shall be my people, and your God, my God. 17Where you die, I will die, and there will I be buried. The Lord do so to me, and more also, if anything but death parts you and me." 18When she saw that she was determined to go with her, she stopped speaking to her.

Ruth was not only willing to change her life, but she clung to Naomi and begged for the change. With this decision came a requirement to change her surroundings. She had to leave the only place she had ever called home to go to another country, away from her family and friends. This may not seem to have anything to do with a spiritual change, but many times, we have to move physically to change spiritually. Ruth could have said she was willing to change all she had ever known, but never actually went with Naomi. When we are willing to change our sin-filled life, the only life we have ever known, to go with God, as Ruth went with Naomi, we must follow through for the change to take place. Now, this does not mean that we have to leave our family or move to another country to be a Christian. This means that the physical changes that must take place are disciplines to change our environment, our attitude, our dealings, and our language, which sums up our sin-filled life. We may even have to change whom we hang out with and where we go for fun. This may seem like too many changes for us to make or we may find it too costly a price to pay.

This is what happened to Orpah, she started to go with Naomi, but when the facts were laid out, it was more than she was willing to change, so she went back to her old life. Some of us have done the same thing to God. We have started to go with Him but when the expectations were laid out before us, we found it too costly a price to pay, and went back to our old life. Change is never easy for any of us, it takes time, and the price we pay is nothing compared to the reward we receive. Orpah broke her relationship with Naomi, unwilling to pay the price of change, and she is never heard from again. Orpah did not receive the benefits of God just because she knew Naomi. She lacked a commitment to continue in the relationship therefore she forfeited her benefits. We do this same thing when we choose not to continue in our relationship with God, even after we said a prayer.

Our physical change is the follow through of our spiritual change. There is a lie that some of us have been taught, "Once you give your life to Christ, you start doing things right because God is leading you." This is a lie that keeps us defeated, because when we don't do things right, we wonder if we truly gave our life to Christ. We constantly question if we are born again, because if we are, then why can't we make better decisions? Have you found yourself at the altar, asking God to forgive and save you week after week? Have you found yourself in a roller-coaster relationship with God? If so, you may have believed this lie, which says that we don't have to physically make any changes to our life, God does it all for you.

There is a joke that many of you may have already heard, but I will share it for those who haven't. There was a flood coming, all the people of this town were evacuating, and one man prayed and asked God to save him from the flood. Some people came by in a car and offered him a ride but he said, "No thank you, God will save me." The waters kept rising and he kept praying. Some people came by in a boat and offered him a ride but he said, "No thank you, God will save me." The waters rose so high that he ended up on the roof of his house and he kept praying. Some people came by in a helicopter and offered him a ride but he said, "No thank you, God will save me." The man drowned and when he stood before the Lord he asked, "Why didn't you save me Lord?" The Lord said, "I sent a car, a boat, and a helicopter, what more did you want me to do?" This is an extreme example but that's what we look like when we sit around thinking God will do everything for us, we just have to pray and believe. Our actions shows our belief and if we believe that all we have to do is sit on the roof-top and God will save us, then we are not acting in faith.

The lie that says, "We start doing everything right because God is leading us," also keeps us immature by causing us to resist the testing of our faith. *"My brethren, count it all joy when you fall into various trials, knowing that the testing of your faith produces patience."* James 1:2-3. According to this Scripture, the various trials that we go through are the testing of our faith. When we resist the trials in our life, we are resisting the changes that God is trying to make in our lives. Many times, we give Satan credit for adversities, when really it is probably God trying to strengthen our faith and build our character. He has to chip the junk out of us, so that we can be more like Him, physically changing our old ways and yielding to Gods ways. *"For My thoughts are not your thoughts, nor are your ways My ways, says the Lord. For as the heavens are higher than the earth, so are My ways higher than your ways, and My thoughts than your thoughts."* Isaiah 55:8-9.

Once we give our life to Christ, the process begins to teach us to be like Christ. If we believe the lie, that we are already like Him because we said a prayer, then we don't hear the truth that we need to change. The result is that we become "holier than thou" in our own self-righteousness. An immature Christian who believes this lie, will act as if they are doing things God's way, but they don't know His ways, nor have they changed to His ways. These self-righteous, immature Christians are also called hypocrites, and many people decide not to become a Christian based on this type of person. So, look at the domino effect that this one lie has on our lives and the lives of those around us. It causes defeat, immaturity, and self-righteousness in believers. It causes non-believes to see Christians as hypocrites, and then they don't desire to know God at all. I can honestly say that I believed this for a while after coming to know the Lord and I really struggled with these same things that I am sharing with you in this chapter.

If this is you today, then you are resisting God and causing others to resist Him too, but you do not have to stay that way. Repent, surrender to His will, grow in the grace and knowledge of Jesus Christ, and allow Him to make changes in you to be more like Him. Life with God is a journey down a straight and narrow path. *"Enter by the narrow gate; for wide is the gate and broad is the way that leads to destruction, and there are many who go in by it. Because narrow is the gate and difficult (confined) is the way which leads to life, and there are few who find it."* Matthew 7:13-14. When we give our life to Christ, through repentance, then we have to learn how to walk down a straight and narrow path, it doesn't come naturally, and it isn't instantaneous. So, it is important to accept being a babe in Christ, so that we can learn and grow, our faith can be tested through various trials, and we can follow through with God. Ruth endured the test, even when offered a way out she stayed the course. She was not only willing, but she followed through to change her surroundings.

Ruth was willing to change her God. Moab was a pagan country and she was brought up to worship Ashtar-Chemosh. While the Moabites adored Chamos as their national god, they also worshipped Ashtar. We were all brought up with some kind of belief that was taught to us by those around us. Whether it was in a church doctrine, a cult, or no foundation at all, we have some belief based on how we were raised. It is hard for those who have no foundation to find truth because there are so many different denominations, religions, and beliefs. With so many denominations to choose from, who knows which one is right. They divide over baptisms, the Holy Spirit, salvation, clothing, gender, and a number of other things. God's word should bring us all together as Christians, but it seems that we are separated by denominations instead of united in Christ. This isn't an easy topic to discuss because many people defend their denomination before they will defend their Lord. Denominations are so prevalent that it is hard to find a church that isn't a denomination. Even non-denominational churches are a denomination in themselves. The name on the building is not the issue; what is being taught inside the building is what counts. *"There is one body and one Spirit, just as you were called in one hope of your calling; one Lord, one faith, one baptism; one God and Father of all, who is above all, and through all, and in you all."* Ephesians 4:4-6. It would be nice if all Christians could lay aside their denominational name and find the one true God, through faith in Jesus Christ, as the Bible teaches and let God work out the rest in each one of us.

Ruth was a woman that was raised with pagan beliefs. She was a part of a religious denomination, but then she finds the one faith that brings her to the one true God, because of Naomi. In the time that Ruth was with Naomi, she probably saw something different about her. She was unlike anyone in her pagan country and it drew her to want more. This is the same for us today; we should be different from the world around us, so that others may be drawn to God. *"You are the salt of the earth; but if the salt loses its flavor, how shall it be seasoned? It is then good for nothing but to be thrown out and trampled underfoot by men."* Matthew 5:13. If you are giving people nothing more than the world gives them, why should they want to know your God?

Our words and actions should be flavorful and appealing, drawing those around us to want to know God. *"You are the light of the world. A city that is set on a hill cannot be hidden."* Matthew 5:14. How are people going to find Christ if you are not lighting the darkness for them to see Him? *"Let your light so shine before men, that they may see your good works and glorify your Father in heaven."* Matthew 5:16. We must be the salt of the earth and light of the world, so that others may see and want God the Father. Ruth found God because of Naomi, and we ourselves, found God because someone showed Him to us. So, are we showing Christ to others in our path? It is important that we are the salt of the earth and the light of the world. If we will let our light shine, Jesus being that light, then others may find Him too and come into a relationship with the Father, just as we have.

Read Ephesians 4:20-32 and answer the questions below.

1. What should you do with your former conduct? _____

2. What does the old man do according to verse 22? _____

_____

_____

3. What does verse 23 say that we should we do with our mind? _____

_____

_____

4. What does the "new man" look like according to verse 24? _____

_____

_____

5. What things in verses 25 & 26 would give opportunity for the devil in your life? __

_____

_____

6. In verse 28 & 29, what would be the person of the old man? _____

_____

_____

7. What would be the person of the new man? _____

_____

_____

8. How would we grieve the Holy Spirit of God, by whom you were sealed for the day of redemption? _____

_____

9. According to verse 32, how should we treat others? _____

_____

_____

10. What changes has God asked you to make in your life to put away the old man? _____

_____

11. Have you completely followed through to see the results in your life? _____

12. How do you think that makes God feel about those who continue in the old man? _____

13. Will you commit to God to follow through with what He is asking you to do and the changes He is asking you to make? _____

Change is a must for any believer it is called repentance. A lifestyle change is required when we give our life to Christ, because we desire to please Him. But even before we believe, we must be willing to change and follow through with that change. Ruth was willing to change and with each change there was a trial, testing her faith to follow through with the change. She was challenged to leave her family and the chance to remarry. She had to give up her beliefs and all she had ever been taught. She had to be willing to become a new person, a day at a time, and a test at a time, leaving the old person behind. Being a Christian isn't easy, but here we have an example of the great blessings that can come if we are willing to change and follow through. Ruth was willing to change and this willingness created a virtuous woman from a pagan worshiper, she let go of her old life for a new one. Just think what God could do with us if we were willing to change.

Chapter 5: Pity Party

Ruth 1:19–2:2

19Now the two of them went until they came to Bethlehem. And it happened, when they had come to Bethlehem, that all the city was excited because of them; and the women said, "Is this Naomi?" 20So she said to them, "Do not call me Naomi (pleasant); call me Mara (bitter), for the Almighty has dealt very bitterly with me. 21I went out full, and the Lord has brought me home again empty. Why do you call me Naomi, since the Lord has testified against me, and the Almighty has afflicted me?" 22So Naomi returned, and Ruth the Moabitess her daughter-in-law with her, who returned from the country of Moab. Now they came to Bethlehem at the beginning of barley harvest. 2:1And Naomi had a kinsman of her husband's, a man of great wealth, of the family of Elimelech; his name was Boaz. 2:2So Ruth the Moabitess said to Naomi, "Please let me go to the field, and glean heads of grain after him in whose sight I may find favor." And she said to her, "Go, my daughter."

Naomi showed unconditional love to Ruth, she was strong in her faith and it showed in her walk. So, what happened to her? She did not seem very strong when they arrived in Bethlehem. She threw a little pity party for herself and invited the whole town to come join her. She changed her name and dramatized her life since she had been gone. She lost her husband, then both of her children, so she had every right to be upset, depressed, and confused. This was a horrible situation and a pity party was fitting for her at this time in her life. She did not understand why God had afflicted her and testified against her, but God had a plan, and it's the bigger picture that no one could see. This is a familiar scene to us because we have all had our own pity party at some point in our life, where the bigger picture of God's plan was invisible to us. Christians are not exempt from having pity parties or from being invited to them. In fact, we are probably more likely to have them because of all the changes that God makes in our life that we don't understand. When we can't see the bigger picture of what God is doing in our life, a pity party may be in the making.

Having a pity party does not disqualify us from heaven; it doesn't cause us to lose our salvation or our relationship with God. A pity party is a natural human reaction to difficulties we go through; however, we should never have a pity party with intentions of staying in the pit. The key to having a successful party is to invite others that will help us out of the pit of our pity. If we don't really want out of the pit, we may find ourselves mad when our friends try to help us out, then maybe we need to check our party purpose. *"An ungodly man digs up evil, and it is on his lips like a burning fire. A perverse man sows strife, and a whisperer separates the best of friends."* Proverbs 16:27-28. We should never allow our pity party to cause strife or contentions; insisting on our own way. *"For where envy and self-seeking exist, confusion and every evil thing will be there."* James 3:16. We should humble ourselves to hear and receive correction, instruction, and guidance from those who love us and care about our walk with God. *"Humble yourselves in the sight of the Lord, and He will lift you up."* James 4:10.

Party Purpose

The party purpose is not for others to climb into the pit with us. We should never have a pity party with intentions to drag others down into the pit. If this is our intention, then we are more likely to invite those people who will tell us how bad they have it, climb into the pit with us, and agree with everything we say even if we are wrong. This kind of pity party will turn into a gossip party, then the pit gets bigger, the gossip gets broader, and everyone is in the pit feeling worse than when the party started. So, if we don't want out of the pit, then our party purpose is to gossip and gain sympathy. *"A fool has no delight in understanding, but in expressing his own heart."* Proverbs 18:2. *"Do not be wise in your own eyes; fear the Lord and depart from evil."* Proverbs 3:7.

The party purpose is not to find answers. We can ask why God allows things to happen in our life, but many times there really are no clear answers. It could be from choices that we have made, from choices that someone else has made, or from situations and circumstances in our life that are beyond our control. The party purpose is to be able to share our feelings, disappointments, or frustrations with those who will encourage, correct, and guide us out of the pit. Stay on track with the party purpose; finding out why is not as important as surrounding ourselves with people that will keep us out of the pit by telling us the truth, holding us accountable, and encouraging us to move forward. Having strong Christian friends who will pray with us, and for us, is what we really need, so the best time to make your invitation list is before a pity party is in the making. Then we know who to invite to the party before our emotions can dictate our list. These pointers will help get us through those tough times when the bigger picture has us in a pity party.

Read Philippians 2:1-8 and answer the questions below.

1. What are the basic foundations of verse 1? _____

2. According to verse 2, how are we to be with others? _____
_____
_____
_____

3. What does verse 3 say? _____
_____
_____
_____

4. What does verse 4 say for us to do for others? _____
_____
_____
_____

5. Who does verse 5 say we should be of the same mind with? _____
_____
_____

6. What's the mind of Christ according to verse 7? _____
_____
_____

7. What's the mind of Christ according to verse 8? _____
_____
_____
_____

8. How can being a servant, humble, and obedient today change our situation
tomorrow? _____
_____
_____
_____
_____

9. How can forgiveness help us escape the pit? _____
_____
_____

Being able to forgive is an important key to unlocking the escape from the pit. You may need to forgive yourself, but forgiveness is still necessary. Remember, forgiveness is a choice not a feeling. When we give forgiveness, we will gain forgiveness.

1. What does Matthew 6:14-15 say. _____

_____

_____

_____

2. Have you been stuck in a pit, with a rollercoaster of emotions? _____

3. Have you been guilty of holding unforgiveness in your heart? _____

Read Matthew 5:43-48 and answer the questions below.

1. What is the command given in verses 43-44? _____

_____

_____

2. Why are we to follow this command, according to verse 45? _____

_____

_____

3. What is Jesus trying to get us to see in verses 46-47 about our behavior? _____

_____

_____

4. What does the word "perfect" mean in verse 48? _____

_____

Partygoers

Being a partygoer is a completely different position than being the one throwing the party. As a partygoer, we must understand the importance of having a successful party for the sake of the one throwing the party. A successful party can be pulled off only if we are in our place as a partygoer. When we ourselves understand the party purpose and accept that there is a bigger picture, then we can better help others out of the pit. Partygoers must be prayerful, faithful, and mature Christians. Partygoers must be led by the Holy Spirit, not by emotions, because the party will be full of some kind of emotion; whether anger, confusion, disappointment, or fear. Emotions will lead us to crawl in the pit with them and we will not be successful to help them out of it. The partygoer plays a very important role at the pity party.

Sometimes their role is just to be an ear to listen and allow the one having the party to cry without any answers. Sometimes their role is to correct and instruct the one having the party in love from Gods word. The partygoer has to allow God to show them which role they are to play while at the party. Either way, the attitude, reactions, and speech of the partygoer will determine the success of the party. They should tell the truth, not be afraid to offend, speak with love and compassion to encourage healing, forgiveness, and acceptance, which can only be done in Christ. *"Let the word of Christ dwell in you richly in all wisdom, teaching and admonishing one another in psalms and hymns and spiritual songs, singing with grace in your hearts to the Lord."* Colossians 3:16.

Read Galatians 5:13-15 and answer the questions below.

1. What does verse 13 say about liberty? _____
_____
_____

2. How are we to serve one another? _____
_____

3. What is the fulfillment of the law according to verse 14? _____
_____
_____

4. How does verse 15 help us be better partygoers? _____
_____
_____
_____

Ruth is a perfect example of the kind of partygoer we should be. She didn't let Naomi's weakness discourage her from believing in Naomi's God. She looked beyond Naomi's pity party to see the person she really was and the God she served. Ruth didn't climb into the pit with her or point a finger at her, she allowed God to move by keeping Naomi in a place of authority in her life. Ruth's confidence in Naomi encouraged her out of the pit. It's amazing what love, respect, and encouragement will do to help someone who is having a pity party find hope. When we allow God to move through us, then others are lifted out of the pits of their life, to see Jesus. We give hope to those who have lost hope, to see Jesus. When we allow God to move, the bigger picture can be played out in their life, not just those in our ladies circle, but also for our husbands, children, and friends because they are the bigger picture in our life.

I have had my fair share of pity parties in my Christian life and have found that when my purpose was to gain sympathy, then I invited the wrong friends, and I stayed in the pit a long time. It is not any fun in the pit, the turmoil, and emotions made me miserable inside and miserable to be around. However, once I found the friend that would tell me the truth, pray with me, and encourage me out of the pit, my party didn't last as long and I found blessings and joy on the other side. I always found that God was working something out of me through each pity party, and learned to have fewer parties and more surrender so the bigger picture could be fulfilled. *"And we know that all things work together for good to those who love God, to those who are the called according to His purpose."* Romans 8:28.

Our lives as Christians should benefit the life of someone else in the bigger picture of God's plan. We are only a piece of the puzzle being put together and sometimes the piece that we are chosen to be is difficult and causes us to have a pity party. This pity party, for Naomi, did not mean she had lost her faith, or that she no longer loved God, just as it doesn't for us when we have our own pity parties. *"...we also glory in tribulations, knowing that tribulation produces perseverance; and perseverance, character, and character, hope."* Romans 5:3-4. While we are in the midst of a tribulation in our life, it is difficult to glory, it is sometimes impossible to look past our emotions to see any good whatsoever. However, on the other side of every tribulation, we will find good that has come of it. Tribulations will build our character, strengthen our faith, and produce fruit in our lives to make us better for tomorrow. *"But now, O Lord, You are our Father; we are the clay, and You our potter; and all we are the work of Your hand."* Isaiah 64:8. If you have never been on the Potter's wheel in your life, then I would encourage you to get born again today, because as Christians we should be experiencing the molding hand of our Father. Allowing God to move in our life is sometimes very hard as we are molded and shaped for His glory, but if we will endure through the tough times, forgive even ourselves, and invite strong Christian friends to any pity parties that arise, then through our surrender, God can do miracles in our life.

Chapter 6: Commitment

Ruth 2:3-7

3Then she left, and went and gleaned in the field after the reapers. And she happened to come to the part of the field belonging to Boaz, who was of the family of Elimelech. 4Now behold, Boaz came from Bethlehem, and said to the reapers, "The Lord be with you!" And they answered him, "The Lord bless you!" 5Then Boaz said to his servant who was in charge of the reapers, "Whose young woman is this?" 6So the servant who was in charge of the reapers answered and said, "It is the young Moabite woman who came back with Naomi from the country of Moab. 7And she said, 'Please let me glean and gather after the reapers among the sheaves.' So she came and has continued from morning until now, though she rested a little in the house."

Ruth showed her integrity as she followed through with the requirements of her commitment to Naomi. Ruth didn't just commit to be with Naomi until they got to Bethlehem, she committed to be with Naomi forever. Ruth and Naomi are alone before they left Moab (Ruth 1:16-17), there was no mention of servants or helpers of any kind. Orpah had already returned, so no one was there to hear Ruth commit, nor did she have anyone there to hold her accountable to follow through. The distance for this journey was 80 to 90 miles over mountainous terrain, which was a long way for anyone, especially two women. Ruth did not bail on Naomi when the road got rough, nor did she allow the hard times they endured cause her to rethink her commitment. Ruth was faithful to her word, she cared for Naomi on this journey, and when they returned she did not look to pawn Naomi off on a relative. She wasted no time finding a way to provide for the two of them and gleaning was something that she could do. This was a form of welfare for the people according to the law given to the children of Israel by God in Lev 19:9-10. Crops were left at the edge of the field for the poor and for strangers. This was not easy work, but Ruth was willing to do whatever she had to for their survival, because she made a commitment, and her integrity caused her to follow through. Naomi didn't have any proof of Ruth's verbal agreement. It was not written on a piece of paper, notarized, and filed at the courthouse, but Ruth stood by her word, no matter what it cost.

It is hard to find people who stand by their word today, even Christians. We talk a big talk about what we can do, but never follow through with the product. We say we will do something, but never do it. Some have even signed that paper, notarized it, and filed it at the courthouse, but still don't follow through. Contracts are not binding and vows are not honored as commitments anymore, we just hire lawyers. We seem to have become a generation of people who can't be trusted. We times when a handshake was binding are definitely past. When I was a kid, my dad worked many long hours and when he came home, he worked side jobs in his small shop. I never questioned why he was gone so much because I didn't know any different. When I look back today, I see my dad as being committed to provide for his family. We may have only had a bowl of beans every night for dinner, but we never went hungry. We didn't have everything we wanted, but we always had what we needed. Even now, at 70 years old, my dad follows through with his commitments, even the ones made with a handshake, because he is a man of his word. It was normal for people to follow through with their commitments 30 years ago, but now, it is difficult to find a man or woman who will stand by their word.

Today, we use the term "no commitment" as a selling point for products and people applaud at the idea of not having to commit. We want to be able to change our mind if we decide we don't want the product tomorrow. We have all made stupid purchases in our life, but hopefully it was a learning experience to be more cautious when making a financial decision. With a "no commitment" selling point, it is hard to learn discipline or self-control, and then we carry the behavior into other areas of our life.

We have all probably experienced the "no show" repairman, the "no show" contractor, and the "no show" appointments. How about the people who don't show up for work or the ones that show up and don't work? The "no commitment" attitude exposes laziness and disrespect in our lives. We make promises we don't keep, not even to our families, or the people we say we love. We make vows that are no good because our word is no good. It seems to be an accepted way of life, even embraced and encouraged. "If you're not happy, then get out." "If you don't want to do that today, then don't." "If you don't want to work there, then quit." How many times have we heard this advice, but never reminded of the commitment we made or encouraged to follow through? The "if it feels good, do it" attitude has consequences that are sometimes very hard to pay. Our society is full of people who have a lack of commitment and it is seen in our work ethics, broken families, and church attendance. Church buildings are shutting down all over because Christians lack commitment in their attendance, tithes, service, and prayer. Christians are refusing the pastors message because it means commitment to change. We have to get back to some basic fundamentals of Christianity with a commitment.

It is sad that Christians have allowed the ways of the world to affect us so deeply. We see a lack of commitment all around us and it is addictive because it's easy. We don't commit because it takes discipline to follow through, and discipline is not easy. This lack of integrity compromises the standards that God has set before us to live by. *"Then Moses spoke to the heads of the tribes concerning the children of Israel, saying, 'This is the thing which the Lord has commanded; If a man vows a vow to the Lord, or swears an oath to bind himself by some agreement, he shall not break his word; he shall do according to all that proceeds out of his mouth.'"* (Numbers 30:1-2) This is a strong commandment and one that God's children have lost. Some will read this and say, "This is the Old Testament, which doesn't apply today." However, the same ones will claim that they are fearfully and wonderfully made (Psalm 139:14), that God has great plans for them (Jer. 29:11), and will give them the desires of their heart (Psalm 37:4). These are all found in the Old Testament too, but these partial verses are beneficial and make us feel good. It seems we want to gain promises that God has given us without the commitment to do our part in the relationship with Him. We expect God to follow through with His promises, but when it comes to the things we promise, then we expect God to understand.

A person who stands by their word, with integrity, is someone who will discipline himself or herself to follow through. Sometimes we are tempted when something better comes along. It is hard to take Aunt Mildred to her hair appointment as you promised when your friends invite you to a fun getaway instead. Sometime things happen and there is no shame in that, but when our lifestyle lacks integrity, we need to examine our heart. Discipline to follow through with our commitments says so much about our Christian walk. When we make a commitment, we should also follow through to see that commitment to the end. Shortly after being born again, I had promised to take pictures at a wedding. When the day arrived to go to the wedding, I did not want to go. I was so very tempted to find a reason why I couldn't make it to the wedding, that's what I would have done before Christ. Then I thought about my testimony as a Christian, and suddenly had compassion on the bride who would be without pictures of her special day. I had to make myself go to the wedding and do the job I promised to do. Through that experience, God really showed me how important it is to follow through with what we commit to do. A lack of follow through shows our lack of commitment, faithfulness, and integrity.

Read Ecclesiastes 5:1-7 and answer the questions below.

1. What is the attitude described in verse 1? _____

_____

2. What is the warning described in verse 2? _____

_____

3. What is the wisdom in verse 3? _____

_____

_____

4. What is the seriousness of verses 4-5? _____

_____

5. What is the result of our lack of discipline in verse 6? _____

_____

_____

6. What is the command in verse 7? _____

_____

_____

There are people who really understand these verses in Ecclesiastes, therefore, they commit to nothing. You never know if you can depend on them to show up to a meeting, or if they will be willing to help you on a project, because they don't give you a straight yes or no. They keep you hanging so that they don't have to make a commitment that will then require them to follow through. Jesus said, *"But let your 'Yes' be 'Yes,' and your 'No,' 'No.' For whatever is more than these is from the evil one."* Matthew 5:37. *"But above all, my brethren, do not swear, either by heaven or by earth or with any other oath. But let your 'Yes' be 'Yes,' and your 'No,' 'No,' lest you fall into judgment."* James 5:12. Having our words match our actions is a standard Christians should live by. Do you wonder what would have happened to Naomi if Ruth had not followed through? What would have happened to Ruth if she had not stood by her commitment? We should think about this for our own life. What is happening to those around us because of our lack of commitment? Isn't it a bad witness of Christ when we claim to be Christians, but look nothing like Him in integrity?

I heard a story once about a boy who promised to rake hay on a Friday night, but when Friday came; his friends wanted him to go to town. When he started to take off to town, his grandpa said, "Didn't you tell that man you would rake hay for him?" The boy said, "Yes sir, but I don't want to, I don't need the money, and I would rather go to town with my friends." Then his grandpa said, "If it costs you everything you have to follow through with your commitment, then you pay it. Money can be replaced, but you can never buy back your reputation. Once you are known as a man who doesn't keep his word, no words will ever change it." The boy followed through with his commitment to the man and never forgot the advice his grandpa gave him. The way we treat others in our commitments shows how we treat God in our commitment to Him. If we will not stand by our word to the people around us, then we won't stand by our word to God.

Read Psalm 37:1-8 and answer the questions below.

1. What promises do you see in these verses? _____
_____

2. What responsibilities are for us to do now? _____
_____
_____

Our life is made up of choices and consequences. The choices we make determine the consequences we receive. If we will choose to commit all our ways to the Lord, then the choices we make will be better because Proverbs 16:3 says, *"Commit your works to the Lord, and your thoughts will be established."*

3. What can you do in your personal life to make better choices? _____
_____
_____

4. What things do you need to commit to the Lord? _____
_____
_____

If we struggle with remembering things then when we make a commitment, we should write it down so that we don't forget. We may also need to get a person that we can trust to be our accountability partner. This should be someone who will remind us to follow through with our commitments. When we do this, we display the integrity of Christ, and integrity will help us be a better witness to others and put us on the right track to becoming a Virtuous Woman, just as Ruth was.

Chapter 7: Integrity

Ruth 2:8-13

8Then Boaz said to Ruth, "You will listen, my daughter, will you not? Do not go to glean in another field, nor go from here, but stay close by my young women. 9Let your eyes be on the field which they reap, and go after them. Have I not commanded the young men not to touch you? And when you are thirsty, go to the vessels and drink from what the young men have drawn." 10Then she fell on her face, bowed down to the ground, and said to him, "Why have I found favor in your eyes, that you should take notice of me, since I am a foreigner?" 11And Boaz answered and said to her, "It has been fully reported to me, all that you have done for your mother-in-law since the death of your husband, and how you have left your father and your mother and the land of your birth, and have come to a people whom you did not know before. 12The Lord repay your work, and a full reward be given you by the Lord God of Israel, under whose wings you have come for refuge." 13Then she said, "Let me find favor in your sight, my lord; for you have comforted me, and have spoken kindly to your maidservant, though I am not like one of your maidservants."

Ruth was a woman of integrity and the result of her integrity began to be seen as God led her to the field of Boaz. Ruth did not set out to find Boaz's field. *"And she happened to come to the part of the field belonging to Boaz."* Ruth 2:3. God led her there and God gave her favor in the sight of Boaz. Boaz gave Ruth permission to glean in his field, not just for that day, but every day. This gave Ruth job security so that she didn't have to search for a place to glean every day all she had to do was follow his reapers. Boaz protected Ruth by commanding his men not to lay their hands on her. She was all alone and it would have been very easy for a man to take advantage of her. With this protection, she could concentrate on gleaning without concern for her personal safety. Boaz gave her substance to keep her healthy. He told her to drink from the water that his men have drawn. She was not his responsibility, she didn't work for him, and she shouldn't have received the benefits of being his employee. However, God gave her favor in the sight of Boaz, so he was compelled to care for her. Ruth had been given job security, protection, and substance from a man she didn't know, but God saw her heart and knew her integrity, therefore God used Boaz to bless her life.

Integrity is the quality of being honest and having strong moral principles or moral uprightness. Integrity is the attribute that drives our decisions and feeds our attitude. The honesty that comes from the core of our heart and the uprightness that comes from the depth of our soul comes from our integrity. Charles R. Swindoll writes in his book, *A Man of Passion & Destiny: David*, "Integrity is what you are when nobody's looking. It means being bone-deep hones."pg.8. A person who possesses integrity has the characteristics of integrity. It is impossible to fake integrity because when we are alone the "real person" comes out. Integrity is the driving force of all that we say and do. It is impossible to pretend to be someone we aren't all the time. We are either a person of integrity or we are a person without integrity and whichever we are will be seen in the characteristics that we display to everyone around us.

1. What does Proverbs 10:9 say about integrity. _____
_____

2. What does Proverbs 11:3 say about integrity. _____
_____

3. What does Proverbs 28:6 say about integrity. _____
_____

4. Why do you think it is so important that we walk in integrity? _____
_____
_____
_____
_____

When Ruth asks Boaz why she has found favor in his sight, look what he says in verse 11. *"It has been fully reported to me, all that you have done for your mother-in-law since the death of your husband, and how you have left your father and your mother and the land of your birth, and have come to a people whom you did not know before. The Lord repay your work and a full reward be given you by the Lord God of Israel, under whose wings you have come for refuge."* Ruth did not light up her own "integrity bill board sign," it was reported to him by someone else. Too many times, we light up our own sign, so others can see that we are good people and see that God is good, and we call it "glorifying God". However, we should, *"Let another man praise you, and not your own mouth; a stranger, and not your own lips."* Proverbs 27:2. God gets more glory when we live our life with integrity without a word. Too much talk, and not enough walk, will turn people away from the God we serve and from us.

Read Proverbs 10:19-22 and answer the questions below.

1. What does verse 19 say about someone who talks a lot? _____

_____

2. What doe verse 19 say about the person who restrains their lips? _____

3. What is the contrast between the righteous and the wicked in verse 20? _____

_____

_____

4. What do the righteous do according to verse 21? _____

_____

5. What happens to the fool in verse 21? _____

_____

Read Philippians 2:1-4 and answer the questions below.

1. What are the four "ifs" mentioned in verse 1? _____

_____

_____

2. What is the result of verse 1, which is listed in verse 2? _____

_____

_____

3. What are the commands given in verse 3 and 4? _____

_____

_____

The things that were reported to Boaz were impressive. Ruth made a sacrifice when she left Moab to follow Naomi. She put herself aside to do what was best for her mother-in-law. She left her own mother, father, friends, and homeland, but Ruth didn't do any of it to impress anyone, she did it because of love and she followed through because of integrity. Our integrity causes us to follow through with the commitments we make to others and to the Lord. If we will commit to the Lord, then the integrity of commitment will be seen in other areas of our life, but the reason people have a lack of commitment is because they lack integrity.

Remember, integrity is what we do when no one is looking. It is what we do when there is nothing to gain. One Christian lady bragged to a friend that she had lied to her boss about being late for work, saying that she had a flat tire rather than the truth that she went back home to get her partial teeth. Wouldn't it be more humiliating to be caught in a lie than to admit the truth about some partial teeth? It seems our integrity is lost as a society of Christians and this lack of integrity causes so many problems in our lives today. When we walk in integrity, however, then our reward comes from the Lord. In Ruth's case, God used a man of integrity to reward the integrity of her heart. It is important for Christians to have integrity, not only so we can benefit from the results as Ruth did, but also that we may be able to deliver the results to someone else, just as Boaz did.

Read Titus 2:7-8 and answer the question below.

1. What is the command for Christians to follow as a lifestyle and to teach others? _

_____

_____

Read Proverbs 2:7-9 and answer the questions below.

1. What does the word "upright" mean? _____

2. What are the benefits from the Lord? _____

_____

_____

Read Proverbs 2:21-22 and answer the question below.

1. What promises do we find for those who walk in integrity? _____

_____

_____

_____

It is important for Christians to walk in integrity. God told Solomon, *"Now if you walk before Me as your father David walked, in integrity of heart and in uprightness, to do according to all that I have commanded you, and if you keep My statutes and My judgments, then I will establish the throne of your kingdom over Israel forever, as I promised David your father, saying, 'You shall not fail to have a man on the throne of Israel.'"* 1 Kings 9:4-5. This promise to Solomon had a condition and the same condition applies to all of us so that God can establish, shield, guard, give, and preserve us. Let's take a few days to examine our attitude and actions to see if we are walking in integrity.

Write down what you found out about your integrity.

_____
_____
_____
_____
_____

If we find that we are not practicing a lifestyle of integrity, then it's time to repent and begin a new life today.

Chapter 8: Compassion

Ruth 2:14-18

14Now Boaz said to her at mealtime, "Come here, and eat of the bread, and dip your piece of bread in the vinegar." So she sat beside the reapers, and he passed parched grain to her; and she ate and was satisfied, and kept some back. 15And when she rose up to glean, Boaz commanded his young men saying, "Let her glean even among the sheaves, and do not reproach her. 16Also let some grain from the bundles fall purposely for her; leave it that she may glean, and do not rebuke her." 17So she gleaned in the field until evening, and beat out what she had gleaned, and it was about an ephah of barley (approx. 31.2lbs). 18Then she took it up and went into the city, and her mother-in-law saw what she had gleaned. So she brought out and gave to her what she had kept back after she had been satisfied.

Boaz had compassion for Ruth which allowed her to gather more barley than if she were gleaning in any other field. His compassion helped nourish her body to continue working and kept her hydrated to do the job. When he invited her to eat, he made her feel welcome by letting her sit at the table with them. Boaz could have given her a piece of bread without inviting her to sit, so it seemed he didn't just want to feed her, but bring her in under his care, and possibly get to know her. He extended his hand repeatedly to her all through Chapter Two, even though he had nothing to gain. In the previous chapter of this study, we see Ruth express her gratitude for all she has been given, and share how he has made her feel saying, *"Let me find favor in your sight, my lord; for you have comforted me, and have spoken kindly to your maidservant, though I am not like one of your maidservants."* Ruth 2:13. She was a foreigner yet compassion was still extended to her and we hear nothing of her beauty. Boaz's actions didn't depend on her heritage, it had nothing to do with her beauty, but it had everything to do with her integrity. When Boaz extended compassion, it encouraged Ruth; it gave her comfort, and made her feel welcome. Sometimes all a person needs is a little compassion to be encouraged.

Compassion literally means, "To suffer together." It is the feeling that arises when we are confronted with another person's suffering and we feel motivated to relieve that suffering. Compassion moves us to take action and that action is kindness. Sometimes we try to be kind without compassion and we end up doing more damage than good. Being kind to someone is not about fulfilling our own needs, but through compassion, fulfills the needs of another person. It has nothing to do with what we want for ourselves or what recognition we get from it. Compassion does not move us to be selfish. It cost Boaz money and time to have compassion and show kindness to Ruth, he did not benefit in any way. He lost money through the barley she gleaned, through the food she ate, and through the men's labor to care for her needs, but because he was moved with compassion to show kindness, he cared more for Ruth than he did for himself. It takes compassion in our heart to be kind to others, without compassion our kindness is self-motivated and not really kindness at all.

There is a lot to be said about a man or woman who is kind. Women like the quality of kindness in a man, and men like this quality in women. *"What is desired in a man is kindness."* Proverbs 19:22. Christians are commanded to put on kindness, *"Therefore, as the elect of God, holy and beloved, put on tender mercies, kindness, humility, meekness, longsuffering,"* Colossians 3:12. Kindness is listed as a fruit of the Spirit in Galatians 5:22-23. Therefore, kindness is commanded by God, it is a fruit of the Holy Spirit, and a desirable quality in character. It doesn't seem that we could go wrong in any way to be kind, but we can get being kind confused with doing good deeds; they look the same on the outside but they are very different on the inside.

So, what is the difference between doing good deeds and being kind? If we look up the definition of these two phrases, we will find they are practically the same; however, good deeds are acts of kindness, which is very different from being kind. Good deeds are not bad; many wonderful things are done by the hands of people doing good deeds. Working through our church or ministry can be a good deed. The most evil and mean person can do good deeds. A person needs only a cause, rally, or emotional stand to do good deeds, but to be kind a person needs compassion in their heart. To be kind is in the nature of a compassionate heart, it doesn't need an emotional stand, a cause, or a rally to move it to be kind. A compassionate person shows an outward display of kindness that comes from their heart toward others. Our heart is where we can find whether we are simply doing good deeds or if we are being kind. Our heart is the most important place to God, because it is the secret place where we dwell with Him, it is where all our treasures are hidden, and were God looks when He sees us. Everything we do and say comes from our heart. *"For where your treasure is, there your heart will be also"* Matthew 6:21.

Boaz had compassion for Ruth and we can see it is not self-motivated because he didn't let her know what he was doing for her. As we see, he told his men to let her glean from as much of the field as she wanted and to even let grain fall from the bundles on purpose for her. This was not said in her presence, he waited for her to go back to work. He was not looking for recognition, just to extend kindness to her in ways she didn't even realize because he had compassion. It was not his intention for her to know, it was only his intention for her to be blessed by being kind to her. We could take some lessons from Boaz when we give to others. If we want people to know what we have done, it is probably because we are actually doing good deeds. Some say they want to share to give God glory but really it is to give glory to them self. Jesus said, *"But when you do a charitable deed, do not let your left hand know what your right hand is doing, that your charitable deed may be in secret; and your Father who sees in secret will Himself reward you openly"* Matthew 6:3-4. This means to keep your acts of kindness to yourself. The genuineness of our heart will be seen whether to receive glory or to bless another with kindness.

Read Matthew 6:1-4 and answer the questions below.

1. What does verse one say about those who do charitable deeds before men? ___
_____

2. Who does verse two say sounds a trumpet? _____

3. Why do they sound the trumpet? _____

4. What is their reward? _____

5. What do we have to do to receive a reward from our Father? _____

6. What does John 12:42-43 say. _____
_____
_____

Read Matthew 6:5-8 and answer the questions below.

1. Have you ever heard someone tell you about when he or she prayed for someone and how that prayer was answered? Why are they doing this according to verse 5? _____

 2. Where is your secret place that the Father sees? _____

Have you ever used big swelling words in your prayer hoping to impress God or someone praying with you? We all probably have once or twice.

3. How can we guard against trying to be impressive with our words? _____

_____

4. How does the Father know the things we have need of before we ask? _____

_____

We can look in our heart and see all that God sees. We can make excuses for our behavior, pump ourselves up, pat our own backs, and ignore our true intentions but it will not change what is in there. God knows the truth and we should want to know the truth also for our own soul sake. Our heart holds the key to all the answers about ourselves. It is important to keep a check on our heart because it can be hurt by others. Many different situations, circumstances, and actions of people can cause us to be hurt. Sometimes we don't even realize that we are hurt until it is too late and our heart grows hard. It grows hard because we build walls to avoid being hurt again.

It is a natural reaction to protect ourselves, but walls cause damage to our relationship with God and our relationship with others. It is impossible to hear God with a hard heart and we do not feel compassion or show kindness with walls of hurt built. All of our hurt is unforgiveness disguised as disappointment, irritation, and even vengeance. We will say things like, "I am just disappointed," or "I am so frustrated" we may even find ourselves joyful at another's misery. Unforgiveness is at the root of all these emotions because of hurt. Hurt can take the form of bitterness, anger, and fear then we find ourselves afraid to be in those situations and possibly begin to avoid people. It is so important to forgive others and ourselves so that our heart can heal. Forgiveness is not easy, it doesn't come naturally, and in some situations, it's not instantaneous. It is a command from God, and our choice to obey but it's only through His love that we are able to forgive.

Read Matthew 18:21-35 and answer the questions below.

1. What three things did the master do in verse 27? _____

_____

_____

2. What action did the servant take in verse 28? _____

_____

_____

3. What does the master say to the servant in verse 33? _____

_____

_____

4. What action does the master take because of the servant's actions in verse 34?_

_____

_____

5. Write out verse 35. Underline where forgiveness takes place. _____

_____

_____

_____

_____

As we read this parable, we see that the servant owed the master such a great debt it would cost him his life, verse 25, *"but as he was not able to pay, his master commanded that he be sold, with his wife and children and all that he had, and that payment be made."* This was a representation of our sin debt to God, yet He forgave us, because we asked. After the servant was forgiven, he found a fellow servant who owed him and publically discredited him. When we don't forgive others, we look like this servant, making all their sins known publically, and hoping for vengeance on their lives. Look at what it does to our witness in verse 31, *"So when his fellow servants saw what had been done, they were very grieved, and came and told their master all that had been done."* God paid a much greater debt for us than anyone could ever be indebted to us for, so regardless of what others say or do, we must keep our hearts pure before the Lord.

When we are filled with compassion, as Jesus was many times for the multitudes, it will be easier for us to forgive those who hurt us. When we have compassion, we can pray for them, whether they need to receive Jesus as Lord or whether they need to repent as Christians. Compassion will overlook others mistakes and understand we are all human. When we can look at people with compassion, then love can be poured out of our hearts to them. *"But when Jesus saw the multitudes, He was moved with compassion for them, because they were weary and scattered, like sheep having no shepherd."* Mathew 9:35. So many are lost and dying while Christians are sitting around watching them die without compassion in their hearts to tell them about Jesus. I can look back to a time in my life that I had no compassion on some of the people in my life and my heart was hard toward them. It really didn't matter what they did or what difficult time they were going through, I still didn't have compassion for them. I figured they were getting what they deserved because of the choices they made; however, I totally overlooked the fact that they didn't know Jesus, and I wasn't a good witness of Him.

It is important to check our heart often and allow God to deal with others and make changes in us as He sees fit. We can't change people or break their heart to repent; only God can do that, we are responsible for our own heart. Their true hearts will be exposed, just as ours has been, and just as Ruth's heart was exposed. As Boaz was moved with compassion and showed kindness to Ruth, she in turn extended it back to Naomi when she kept back food for her. Ruth wasn't asking for any handouts, she was just being faithful and was willing to work for what she got. She didn't seek any gifts only a place to glean so that she could care for Naomi and herself. She didn't ask for any food, but when it was given to her, she gave to Naomi also. We can be sure that Ruth was not perfect and neither was Naomi but having compassion has nothing to do with the perfection of others. Having compassion is to realize that we all make mistakes and none of us is perfect. It is remembering that you were once lost and had to ask for forgiveness. We still make mistakes, even as Christians and we want to be forgiven. Everyone's heart will be exposed at some point but it's not our job to do the exposing. *"Hatred stirs up strife, but love covers all sins."* Proverbs 10:12 So, let's just be sure we don't allow unforgiveness to keep us from the greatest relationship we could ever have with our heavenly Father that we may allow His love to fill our hearts, His joy to make us full, and the compassion for others to know Him complete our lives.

Chapter 9: Respect

Ruth 2:19-23

19And her mother-in-law said to her, "Where have you gleaned today? And where did you work? Blessed be the one who took notice of you." So she told her mother-in-law with whom she had worked, and said, "The man's name with whom I worked today is Boaz." 20Then Naomi said to her daughter-in-law, "Blessed be he of the Lord, who has not forsaken His kindness to the living and the dead!" And Naomi said to her, "The man is a relative of ours, one of our near kinsmen." 21Then Ruth the Moabitess said, "He also said to me, 'You shall stay close by my young men until they have finished all my harvest.'" 22And Naomi said to Ruth her daughter-in-law, "It is good, my daughter, that you go out with his young women, and that people do not meet you in any other field." 23So she stayed close by the young women of Boaz, to glean until the end of the barley harvest and wheat harvest; and she dwelt with her mother-in-law.

Naomi and Ruth had a relationship of respect. They were courteous and kind to each other. They both encouraged the other in goodness. Ruth was not resentful toward Naomi for having to work all day in the field. She came home and shared with Naomi, not only food, but a report of her day. Naomi didn't act superior, as if Ruth owed her something. She was genuinely interested in her day and rejoiced in what God did for them through Ruth's faithfulness. Each of these ladies respected the others position in the family and each one of their jobs was important. Through this respect and love for one another, they opened a door of communication. Ruth listened to Naomi's advice and followed her instruction because she respected her. They found the key to what is missing in most relationships today, from friends to marriages; every relationship should have love and respect as a main ingredient.

It is hard to find good friends today because it seems to be more about what we can gain from the relationship than what we can give, which stems from a lack of love and respect. Husbands and wives are fighting for respect and love, without honest and open communication. With the economy in such bad shape these days, both husband and wife are in the work force, and it seems to be a struggle for who is responsible for dinner, dishes, laundry, child care, homework, grocery shopping, and the list goes on. One or both spouses feel unappreciated for their contribution to the family but neither of them knows how to share how they feel.

These feelings come out in our attitude and actions. We will find ourselves so mad at our spouse for some of the dumbest things. They don't understand why we are mad and we don't either, but if we take the roadmap back, most generally we would find that it stems from feelings we bottled up inside because we lack open honest communication in our relationship. In years of ministry and some personal experience, I have found that spouses are fearful of being hurt, laughed at, or controlled. So, in fear, we close our mouth and hide it all inside.

Communication is a vital part of any relationship and is the key to its success or failure. With that said, it is important that we know how to communicate. Communicating is not just about opening our mouth and letting everything out, it's about knowing how to speak to someone with respect and love. We can do all kinds of talking yet never communicate a single thing. My husband used to tell me that it was not *what* I said but *how* I said it. I would get so mad at him because I really didn't understand what he was talking about; he said I was talking *at* him, instead of *to* him. I didn't have respect for him as my husband so when I spoke all he could hear was the disrespect behind my voice.

In a marriage of 20 years, unfulfilled expectations had taken its toll and disrespect was underlining everything I said and did. I wanted to communicate with him but every time we talked it ended in an argument so he avoided conversations like the plague. I really thought that he was the one with the problem until God showed me that I had built walls of disappointment. He brought to my memory all the times I had said, "I'm disappointed," all the times I had felt disappointed, and my mind was full of so much that it brought me to tears. In my brokenness, God showed me that my wall of disappointment was really unforgiveness in disguise. It didn't sound like a bad thing to be disappointed, however, to say I was holding unforgiveness in my heart sounded horrible. I didn't realize that each pretty little box of disappointment was building a wall that hardened my heart toward God, my husband, and others in my life. I had to ask God to forgive me, my husband to forgive me, and I made my journey through phone calls and home visits to ask for forgiveness from others.

Unforgiveness disguised as disappointment had overshadowed all the good in my life. It caused me to focus on the past and never give my husband a chance to gain the respect that he deserved. I saw all the wrongs that he did and none of the things he did right. With my wall destroyed, I began to notice a difference in how my husband responded to me. Our conversations didn't end up in arguments and he began to talk to me, as well as communicate with me. Something I had wanted so desperately, for so long had finally become a reality because I allowed forgiveness to heal my heart. How we speak to people is so important. Ruth and

Naomi respected each other, respected the other's position and responsibilities in the family, and as a result, they had open and honest communication. *"Nevertheless let each one of you in particular so love his own wife as himself, and let the wife see that she respects her husband."* Ephesians 5:33. Many of us take this Scripture and place the blame on our husbands, saying, "He doesn't love me as Christ loved the church so why should I respect him?"

Read 1 Peter 3:1-6 and answer the questions below.

1. What does verse 1 say we are to do as wives? _____

_____

_____

2. According to verse 1, what could happen to our husbands? _____

_____

_____

3. What does verse 2 mean? _____

_____

_____

4. Which verse, 3 or 4, is the most beautiful to God? _____
Why _____

_____

5. How did holy women adorn themselves in old times? _____

_____

_____

These scriptures are not easy to swallow when you are in a marriage where your spouse is unsaved or uncommitted. However, if we read a little farther we will find more encouragement on how to be successful in our behavior.

Read 1 Peter 3:8-17 and answer the questions below.

1. What 5 things are mentioned in verse 8 that will help us? _____

_____

_____

2. What must we do to inherit a blessing according to verse 9? _____

_____

3. What are the commands listed in verses 10 and 11? _____

_____

4. What are the rewards listed in verse 12? _____

_____

_____

5. What encouragement do you find in verses 13 through 17? _____

_____

_____

_____

6. How can you apply 1 Peter Chapter Three to your life? _____

_____

_____

_____

_____

Even though Ruth and Naomi were not married or in an intimate relationship, they were a perfect example of how we should treat each other with respect and love. Just remember this: "it begins with me." We don't have to wait for our husband's to treat us the way we want to be treated, we can begin to treat them with respect, and watch things change. It won't happen in your first attempt and it won't happen overnight, but change will happen if you will stay consistent to show them respect even if they don't show you love. One of the hardest things for us to do is to let go of what we want them to do for us and give them what they need. Our first response to this statement is, "What about my needs?" Set your heart to give him respect and see if 1 Peter 3 does not prove to be right. Let your conduct be chaste and accompanied by fear of the Lord. Let your beauty be the hidden person of the heart, with the incorruptible ornament of a gentle and quiet spirit, which is very precious in the sight of God. Don't return evil for evil, refrain your tongue from evil, seek peace, and pursue it. Sanctify the Lord God in your heart, and remember: "it begins with me."

Chapter 10: Obedience

Ruth 3:1-6

1Then Naomi her mother-in-law said to her, "My daughter, shall I not seek security for you, that it may be well with you? 2Now Boaz, whose young women you were with, is he not our kinsman? In fact, he is winnowing barley tonight at the threshing floor. 3Therefore wash yourself and anoint yourself, put on your best garment and go down to the threshing floor, but do not make yourself known to the man until he has finished eating and drinking. 4Then it shall be, when he lies down, that you shall notice the place where he lies, and you shall go in, uncover his feet, and lie down; and he will tell you what you should do." 5And she said to her, "All that you say to me I will do." 6So she went down to the threshing floor and did according to all that her mother-in-law instructed her.

Ruth obeyed the voice of Naomi in everything she told her to do, without question, without backtalk, or shortcut. Obedience is such a difficult subject for adults. We don't mind talking about it when we are discussing our kids, but we don't want to talk about the importance of it for ourselves. Why is it so difficult for adults to obey? We spend the first several years of our life being told what to do, and once we are out on our own, we don't want to be told what to do anymore. We want to be in charge of our own life and our own destiny. We want to make our own mistakes and experience our own failures. It begins for most of us in our teenage years with rebellion and can continue into our adult years if we do not get grounded in some understanding of truth and respect for authority. Rebellion is rampant all over the world today, not only with teenagers but also with adults. It is happening between parents and children, police and citizens, even pastors and congregations. *"For rebellion is as the sin of witchcraft, and stubbornness is as iniquity and idolatry. Because thou hast rejected the word of the Lord, He hath also rejected thee from being king."* 1 Samuel 15:23. This is what the Lord spoke through Samuel to King Saul, but the same could be said of us if we are in rebellion.

Obedience is a hard pill to swallow and is our biggest struggle as an adult Christian. The older we get the more we believe we have life figured out and the harder it is to be taught. It's been said, "It's hard to teach an old dog new tricks," but no matter how much education we have or how many years we have lived, we should never think of ourselves as beyond being taught. When we learn something, we gain knowledge. When we put knowledge into practice, we have gained wisdom. A wise person is an obedient Christian. *"But why do you call Me 'Lord, Lord,' and do not do the things which I say? Whoever comes to Me, and hears My sayings and does them, I will show you whom he is like: He is like a man building a house, who dug deep and laid the foundation on the rock. And when the flood arose, the stream beat vehemently against that house, and could not shake it, for it was founded on the rock."* Luke 6:46-48. *"The fear of the Lord is the beginning of knowledge; but fools despise wisdom and instruction."* Proverbs 1:7

Being teachable is so important in our Christian walk. We do not rise up from our salvation prayer with all the answers about how to be a Christian. Before that moment, we lived our life walking down the broad path that leads to destruction but now we must learn how to walk down the narrow path that is life. *"Enter by the narrow gate; for wide is the gate and broad is the way that leads to destruction, and there are many who go in by it. Because narrow is the gate and confined is the way which leads to life, and there are few who find it."* Matthew 7:13-14. Unless we are teachable, we will resist all the instruction and guidance to walk the narrow way. We will reject God and His ways for our life. Ruth was teachable, not rebellious, or prideful. She listened to Naomi and followed her instructions. This may not be how Ruth thought her life would end up; widowed, in a foreign country, gleaning in the fields but she didn't allow any of it to harden her heart and become disobedient.

Obedience requires us to lay aside what we think or how we feel and just obey what we may not even understand because God's ways are not our ways according to Isaiah 55:8-9. God uses many ways to speak to us and when He does, we must obey. Just as Ruth's instruction and guidance came from Naomi, ours may come from our husband, pastor, Sunday school teacher, or a mature Christian in our life. Most of the time we don't want to be told what to do by another human being, we just want God to open up heaven and speak to us directly, and most importantly, in private. We don't want the humiliation and embarrassment of someone telling us that what we are doing or saying is wrong.

Pride and rebellion is how Korah responded to Moses in Numbers 16. Korah and a group of leaders rose up against Moses and Aaron saying, *"You take too much upon yourselves, for all the congregation is holy, every one of them, and the Lord is among them. Why then do you exalt yourselves above the congregation of the Lord?"* vs. 3. Korah didn't respect the position of authority that God placed in Moses. He caused a large group of people to rise up against Moses too. Korah's actions cost him his life, his family, and all the men that were with him. *"So they and all those with them went down alive into the pit; the earth closed over them, and they perished from among the congregation"* Numbers 16:33. The people that continued to murmur against Moses after Korah's death were killed by God with a plague.

Read Numbers 16:1-50 and answer the questions below.

1. Think about your own life, have you been a Korah or followed a Korah? _____

2. Is God talking to you about your rebellion and disobedience? _____

3. Do you struggle with authority in your life? _____

4. Would you repent if you knew God was going to do to you what He did to Korah?
_____

Korah wanted to be a boss so he didn't have to take orders, instruction, or correction from Moses. If we look at our society today, it looks much like this, everyone wants to be the boss or be in charge to give orders, but no one wants to be ordered or bossed. This has overflowed into Christianity; we have people, who are not set apart by God, telling pastors, who are set apart by God, what to do and what to preach. We seem to want to set ourselves in places we are not qualified for, just to keep from being told what to do. We have such a rebellious nature as humans that it seems so natural to say, "No one is going to tell me what to do" and women have one they like to use, "No *man* is going to tell me what to do." With this attitude, we disregard the probability that God is using our pastor, teachers, husband, or friends to speak to us. If we research Scriptures, we will find that many prophets were killed by the hands of people who claimed to know God. We should be careful and take the advice given by Gamaliel.

Read Acts 5:33-42 and answer the questions below.

1. Who are the religious people are furious with according to the previous verses.
_____
_____

2. What was the advice Gamaliel gave to the high priest and all who were with him? _____
_____

3. What did they do to the apostles despite the advice given? _____
_____
_____

4. How did the apostles respond? _____

_____

_____

Obedience had nothing to do with how the apostles felt or what blessings they received; their obedience was because they loved God. *"Then Peter and the other apostles answered and said: We ought to obey God rather than men. The God of our fathers raised up Jesus who you murdered by hanging on a tree. Him God has exalted to His right hand to be Prince and Savior, to give repentance to Israel and forgiveness of sins. And we are His witnesses to these things and so also is the Holy Spirit whom God has given to those who obey Him"* Acts 5:29-32. As Peter preached, it wasn't a very nice message to the "church people," but he offered a way for them to receive; repent and obey, but instead, they acted just as we do, "slay the messenger!" Rejecting God's word is rejecting God Himself. When we refuse to hear that we need to change, we refuse to grow in the Lord. If we slay the messenger of the Lord, our consequences could be the same as Korah. We can't let our emotions of how we feel or ideas of what we think get in the way of our obedience to God. God's word is what we must obey, no matter who brings it to our attention. We should never set ourselves in a position of authority over whom God has set in place. *"A wise son heeds his father's instruction, but a scoffer does not listen to rebuke"* Proverbs 13:1.

Read Romans 13:1-4 and answer the questions below.

1. Who should be subject to the governing authorities? _____

2. Who set authorities in place and appoints them? _____

3. What happens to those who resist? _____

4. What is the key to getting along with authority? _____

5. Write and explain verse 4. _____

_____

_____

_____

_____

_____

_____

_____

6. What does Hebrews 13:7 say? _____

_____

_____

_____

_____

7. What does Hebrews 13:17 say? _____

_____

_____

_____

_____

_____

"If you are willing and obedient, you shall eat of the good of the land; but if you refuse and rebel, you shall be devoured by the sword; for the mouth of the Lord has spoken." Isaiah 1:19-20 These words of the Lord are very clear about what will happen to us if we choose to refuse and rebel against Him, and very clear what we will receive if we are willing and obedient. God does not leave us needing to ask Him any questions about this passage, but we do need to ask ourselves if we are willing and obedient or refusing and rebellious? If you don't like the answer, then repent and obey.

Chapter 11: Wisdom

Ruth 3:7-13

7And after Boaz had eaten and drunk, and his heart was cheerful, he went to lie down at the end of the heap of grain; and she came softly, uncovered his feet, and lay down. 8Now it happened at midnight that the man was startled, and turned himself; and there, a woman was lying at his feet. 9And he said, "Who are you?" so she answered, "I am Ruth, your maidservant. Take your maidservant under your wing, for you are a near kinsman." 10Then he said, "Blessed are you of the Lord, my daughter! For you have shown more kindness at the end than at the beginning, in that you did not go after young men, whether poor or rich. 11And now my daughter, do not fear, I will do for you all that you request, for all the people of my town know that you are a virtuous woman. 12Now it is true that I am your near kinsman; however, there is a kinsman nearer than I. 13Stay this night, and in the morning it shall be that if he will perform the duty of a near kinsman for you good; let him do it. But if he does not want to perform the duty for you, then I will perform the duty for you, as the Lord lives! Lie down until morning."

Naomi was very wise in her instructions and Ruth was very wise to follow them. Neither of these ladies moved in their emotions. Each detail of the instructions had a purpose and it was very important that Ruth follow them to the letter. First, she was to wait until Boaz had finished eating and drinking, and then let him lie down before she went to him. At the end of the day, he was tired, hungry, and needed some rest. It would *not* have been wise for Ruth to go to him as soon as he finished working or interrupt him in the middle of his job.

Today, many wives make this mistake, we have something we want to say or a situation we need to discuss, but we don't wait for the right time. Giving Boaz time to eat and rest was very important to show respect for him. We need to give our husbands time to eat and rest before we hit them with any situation. We need to resist the temptation to blurt out whatever is on our mind at the very moment it is there. Cell phones and social media have fed our need to say what we want to say, when we want to say it. It is something we get use to and it becomes a hard habit to break. My husband carried a cell phone for years, recently he shut it off, and it has been difficult to get used to it. I could call him anytime I had a question or needed to tell him something. Now, I have to wait until I see him. I have learned that some things I called him about really weren't that important and to be patient about the other things that are. Interrupting his day with questions and information made it difficult for him to get his job done. Now, at the end of the day, we can sit down and talk about things together.

Another reason it is a good idea to give our husbands time after work is because when we speak, we want them to listen and be attentive to what we say. When we speak too soon, it could cause an argument, misunderstandings, or hurt feelings because of the lack of ability to be attentive. We need to give them the same respect that we want for ourselves so it is important that we do not interrupt what they are saying or change the subject in the middle of the conversation. This happens when we are not listening to them or not interested in what they are saying. Sometimes our minds wander off and it shows in our responses, which makes them feel as if we don't care. When we stay focused and discipline ourselves to listen to them, it strengthens their confidence and encourages them. They will find assurance in the relationship and we should want to do that for them, just as we want it done for us.

In our culture today, we have husbands and wives in the work place, so most of the time wives are not at home waiting for their husbands with dinner on the table, as in the days of the Cleavers in the sitcom "Leave it to Beaver". It is more likely that they are coming in at different times or one may be leaving while the other is coming home. This makes the time for communication more challenging. We take opportunities to speak when we have the chance rather than when it's the right time. Our schedules cause us to think about what is convenient rather than what is best for the other person. We are not trying to be disrespectful or insensitive; we just don't have the time to be thoughtful. If this is the case in your life, then find a common time when you both agree to talk about anything you have going on. Rather than hitting each other with the unexpected. This way, you both know that at a certain time during the day, you are able to share whatever needs you have or situations that need to be discussed. There may be ways to change your schedules or some things you can cut out of your schedules so that you have more time together. These are things to pray about with each other.

Another struggle some husbands and wives have is the type of work they do. My husband and I both work together as a family unit. I'm a homemaker along with the ministry duties of writing books and recording/editing our radio programs so I spend a lot of time at a computer. He works hard physically everyday to provide for our family. At the end of the day, we are both tired. Even though I don't do much physical work, the mental work I do causes my body to be tired. We went through a period of time when we argued because he could not understand why I was tired when all I did was sit at a desk all day. He wasn't being mean, he just didn't understand. As I have ministered to women, I found that many of them in the workforce have this same problem, their office job causes their bodies to be physically tired, and their husbands, who work physically, do not understand. I had to learn to be wise with this situation, because it was not worth being at odds about. Instead of getting upset with him for not understanding that I was tired, I just accepted that we are different and began to show him respect in his need for rest. As I did this, he in turn, has had compassion on me. He still doesn't understand, but it is no longer an issue in our home. We may not like the way things are in our lives, but with a little wisdom, we can feel better about our lives no matter what we are going through.

Ruth's next instruction was to uncover his feet and lie down. By doing this, Ruth showed her total submission to Boaz. She was there to claim her right to be redeemed, but she did it with humility, not with arrogance that demanded her rights. Women today are taught to demand their rights, and to stand toe to toe with the one in which we mean to get them. We are so afraid that we will not be loved or respected if we don't demand our right to be. We reject the idea of submission out of fear of being controlled or taken advantage of by others. We can get so concerned about our rights, that we forget the rights of others. Ruth's right to be redeemed will be a great cost Boaz.

Sometimes we forget that our rights may be at the cost of someone else's rights. Ruth was laying herself at the mercy of Boaz, it was his decision to fulfill his responsibility to redeem her or not. She was not demanding that right, she was humbly asking for that right. Boaz let her know that this involved other people and would affect their lives. This would have to be brought to the attention of the closer relative then a decision could be made. Without Naomi's wise counsel, Ruth would not have known what to say or do. This is the problem with many of our young ladies today; they have not been given wise counsel in how to conduct themselves. They are demanding things they think they have a right to and moving within their emotions. Some of the things they are demanding as a right are actually ruining their life instead of making it better. As Christian women, we need to be giving wise counsel as well as seeking it for ourselves.

Read Titus 2:3-5 and answer the questions below.

1. The word "likewise" refers back to verse 2, what are the instructions given there?

_____

_____

2. List the instructions found in verse 3. _____

_____

3. What are we to teach others according to verse 4-5? _____

_____

_____

4. According to verse 5, why are these teachings so important? _____

_____

_____

It is important that we know what God's word says for our lives, what He expects from us as Christians, and to hold ourselves accountable to His word. Wisdom is defined as the right use or exercise of knowledge. Knowledge comes as we read and hear His word. Wisdom is gained when we receive and apply His word to our life with understanding. If we are not reading and hearing His word, we cannot receive and apply His truths. *"A wise man will hear and increase learning, and a man of understanding will attain wise counsel"* Proverbs 1:5. The wisdom that the Lord gives is deeper and more meaningful than the wisdom that we receive in our experiences of life and book studies. Man can study the Bible and seek for knowledge, but without receiving and applying it to their own life, and they will not gain wisdom. *"For the Lord gives wisdom; from His mouth come knowledge and understanding"* Proverbs 2:6. This kind of wisdom is from the root word khawkam, which means to be wise. Being wise is much deeper than having wisdom. We can gain wisdom in areas of life, but to be wise covers the entire person. *"Do not be wise in your own eyes; fear the Lord and depart from evil"* Proverbs 3:7 This wisdom can only come from above and is attained when we listen to instruction, give attention to know understanding and keep His commands in our heart. *"Wisdom is the principal thing; therefore get wisdom and in all your getting, get understanding"* Proverbs 4:7

Read Deuteronomy 4:5-9 and answer the questions below.

1. The first part of verse 5 says they were taught what the Lord commanded. What does the last part of verse 5 say they are to do? _____

2. What does verse 6 say is their wisdom and understanding? _____

_____

3. What will the people say about them according to verse 6? _____

4. What truth does verse 7 say about God? _____

_____

5. What truth does verse 8 say about God's statutes? _____
_____

6. What warning is given in verse 9? _____
_____

7. What command is given in verse 9? _____

God clearly shows us in His word what it means to be wise. The key for us today is to receive Jesus Christ as our Lord and Savior, then we will receive the Holy Spirit who will teach us all things, bring to remembrance all things that Jesus said according to John 14:26, and guide us into all truth according to John 16:13. Ruth has been taught by Naomi and instructed by Boaz and she was wisely obeying all she was told to do. Boaz shared with her that his willingness to redeem her came from the fact that she was a virtuous woman. Her virtue was seen in her actions of obedience, integrity of her word, and respect to authority. Boaz was not the only one who saw it, he said, *"For all the people of my town know that you are a virtuous woman."* The genuineness of her heart was seen in her deeds, heard in her words, and witnessed in her attitude by everyone in town. Proverbs describes the virtuous woman as being wise. *"She opens her mouth with wisdom, and on her tongue is the law of kindness"* Proverbs 31:26. We don't have to have a degree on the wall or have post-nominal abbreviations after our name to be considered wise; we just need to be virtuous.

Chapter 12: Endurance

Ruth 3:14-18

14So she lay at his feet until morning, and she arose before one could recognize another. Then he said, "Do not let it be known that the woman came to the threshing floor." 15Also he said, "Bring the shawl that is on you and hold it." And when she held it, he measured six ephahs of barley, and laid it on her. Then she went into the city. 16So when she came to her mother-in-law, she said, "Is that you, my daughter?" Then she told her all that the man had done for her. 17And she said, "These six ephahs of barley he gave me; for he said to me, 'Do not go empty-handed to your mother-in-law.'" 18Then she said, "Sit still, my daughter, until you know how the matter will turn out; for the man will not rest until he has concluded the matter this day."

Ruth probably hoped for a different answer than what she received. She had built a relationship with Boaz, even though it was not an intimate one; it was more than she had with the man who was a closer relative. She may be redeemed by a man she doesn't know, and I would imagine that her heart was set on Boaz. He had shown kindness to her with his words and actions. He had complimented her on more than one occasion and continually provided substance for her and Naomi. He had protected her from harm in the field, and in these verses, he was protecting her reputation. He was a dream man to any woman who was on the receiving end of such treatment. He was a godly man who respected others, he worked hard with integrity, he was kind, and compassionate. Under the circumstances, it may have been difficult for her to walk away knowing that she may have to marry another man but she couldn't do anything about it. This seems ridiculous to us today; women who have been liberated, that there would be nothing that we could do if we were put in the same situation. But, if we can look past the "marriage" part of this, we will see that we are put in these same situations; ones that require us to be patient and endure.

Many times, we are so focused on what we want, and we will do whatever it takes to make it happen. We will manipulate others to get our way and we do it by any means necessary. Some of us may be offended at the very thought that we would use manipulation to get our way, but the truth is, we can use it without even thinking out a strategic plan. A natural human instinct of survival can cause us to be devious and cunning. A natural human desire can cause us to do the same.

Manipulation can be as blatant as a lie or as subtle as a cry, it is when we allow our feeling or desires cloud the judgment of our attitude and integrity. It comes out when we allow the part of us that is in desperate need to control the destiny of our life overtake us. We may look a lot like Jezebel when we are in this state. To think that we are acting like Jezebel may be a little harsh or extreme, but what if there is a little Jezebel in all of us.

Giving into the temptations to release the Jezebel inside of us will only allow that part of us to grow stronger, so we must fight. It's like the old wise tale of the two dogs that has been attributed to a Native American Elder, who used it to describe his own inner struggles. There are several versions of this story that have been used in books and movies. Some versions use two dogs others have used two wolves but the basic story is this: Inside of you are two dogs, one is evil, and the other is good. The evil dog fights the good dog all the time. Whichever one you feed the most will win. Rev. Billy Graham used a version of this story to describe the warfare that goes on inside a person who is born again on page 92 of his book, *The Holy Spirit: Activating God's Power in Your Life.* Rev. Graham says, "We have two natures within us, both struggling for mastery. Which one will dominate us? It depends on which one we feed." We can learn a few things about Jezebel that will help us recognize when she is rising up in us. Knowing these things will teach us how to deny her food.

Read 1 Kings 21:7-10 and answer the questions below.

1. What is the first thing she says to Ahab in verse 7? _____
_____

2. What is the next thing she tells him to do in verse 7? _____
_____

3. What is the last thing she says in verse 7? _____
_____

4. What authority did she use in verse 8 to get the job done? _____
_____

In verse 7, we see into the heart of Jezebel. She made fun of Ahab for not getting what he wanted. He was not only her husband, but he was also the king! However, he didn't exercise the authority of either of those positions in her life? Jezebel continued to humiliate him by letting him know that she was capable of getting things done, all he needed to do was go eat, drink, and rest assured that she would deliver. This behavior is known as emasculation, which is *to deprive a man of his masculine strength or vigor* (Webster's Dictionary).

Now, this does not mean that we don't love our husband, or that we are evil like Jezebel. Emasculation happens when we act toward him the same way Jezebel did, whether we do that in ignorance, anger, frustration, or desire for our own way. This is not to say that we have to shut our mouth and be a robot while our husband does everything and makes all the decisions. This is about being a help meet with him in all things, to listen as well as speak, and allow him to lead, even when it's not our way.

Ahab was Jezebel's mouthpiece; he did what she told him to do. He had the title of king but she was in control of the country. There is a funny little joke that many people tell that goes like this: "My husband wears the pants in the family; I just tell him which ones to wear." This really isn't a joke in many marriages today. We act like it is no big deal but it is another way we emasculate our husbands and cause them to sin against God as the spiritual leader of our home. King Ahab had a responsibility to God to lead the country in God's ways, but he allowed Jezebel to lead him instead. This same responsibility is on our husband to lead the family in God's ways. If we become his mouthpiece, we could hurt his relationship with God.

This is where we run into the question of an unbelieving husband, which takes us to 1 Peter 3:1-5, read it again. If you have an unbelieving husband, this is a good verse to meditate on continually. We have to keep our own behavior in check and be a witness to them in the things we say and do, how we respond to situations, and keeping God first in our life. It is important that in the process of being a witness we don't become condemning. We can do that if we will focus more on our relationship with God and less on how we can be a witness. The witnessing will come naturally, as we live our life as Christ, in obedience to the Father.

The evil that Jezebel did is probably beyond what any of us are really capable of, but her intentions behind why she did these things could be something we fight every day. She desired power, control, position, and prestige; she was bossy, controlling, deceitful, and manipulative. She thought about what she could gain in every situation and believed she was always right. None of us want to admit to being like her in any way, shape, or form, but we should admit if we have had any of these characteristics, so that we can be aware of what we need to repent of and fight against it in the future. God has given us everything we need to be successful in our Christian walk. He has given us an example of a virtuous woman in Ruth and He has given us an example of what we are fighting in Jezebel. It is hard when we see ourselves in someone like Jezebel and our first response is to reject that we see it at all, but let's not deceive ourselves, repent and allow God to change us.

Take some time to evaluate yourself and prayerfully consider the answers to these questions.

1. Have you ever made fun of your husband or humiliated him? _____

2. Have you ever let him know that you can do a better job than he can do, with anything? _____

3. Have you ever told your husband what to do? _____

4. Have you been guilty of using his position for your own gain? _____

5. What Jezebel characteristics do you need to repent of? _____

_____

_____

_____

_____

_____

I fed the Jezebel inside of me during a period of my life. Some of it was done in ignorance, but other times I did it in anger and arrogance. After my husband and I were married for two years, he took a job that required him to be gone for six weeks at a time, then home for one week. He had October through December at home then he was gone on schedule again. There were some changes over the 17 years in his line of work with promotions that allowed him to be home more and opportunities for me to go with him, but we didn't have a normal life. With him being gone, I had to take charge of everything at home. Most decisions I had to make on my own or be the mouthpiece when the decisions were made. The more I was in this position, the less I needed him to help me, and the more I let him know. Now, I am not making an excuse for myself, I am simply "setting the stage" for what brought me to arrogance and anger. My ignorance came from not knowing Jesus Christ as my Lord for the first 9 years of our marriage, my anger came from being alone, and my arrogance came from being in that position. I eventually let him know that I could make things happen, do things better, and knew what was best for *my* family. As I saw myself in Jezebel, I had to repent and ask God to forgive me, I also asked my husband to forgive me. Then I had to learn to submit to him and make changes in my behavior. After so many years of pointing out all his faults and failures, he needed encouragement. I started lifting him up with compliments and encouraging him with love. It took some time for healing to take place in our hearts but through prayer and patience, we endured.

To endure with patience is probably the most difficult thing anyone can do and without prayer, it is impossible. The dictionary definition of endurance is *a continuing under pain or distress without sinking or yielding to the pressure.* The definition of patience is *the suffering of afflictions with a calm unruffled temper.* A good word that sums the two of these together is long-suffering, which is long endurance, patience of offense, and is a fruit of the Spirit, found in Galatians 5:22-23. This brings a whole new understanding of the term "patience is a virtue." Enduring this time of uncertainty could not have been easy for Ruth, but it does show her virtuous, fruitful character. Contrary to popular belief, we should pray for patience, it would help us go through trials and tribulations with a calm, unruffled temper, and be a testimony to others. When we build our relationship with God through prayer and Bible study, we will gain understanding of who He is and what He expects from us, then we will gain confidence to trust Him.

Read Proverbs 3:1-10 and answer the questions below.

1. According to verse 2, what are the results of verse 1? _____
_____

2. What must we do according to verse 3 to receive the promise of verse 4? _____
_____
_____

3. Write and memorize verses 5-6 to help patience become a virtue in your life. ___
_____
_____

4. What does verse 7 say we must do before verse 8 can be given? _____
_____

5. According to verse 9, what must we do to receive the promise of verse 10? ____
_____
_____

Jesus said, *"And all things, whatsoever ye shall ask in prayer, believing, ye shall receive"* Matthew 21:22. To receive the things we ask for in prayer, we must believe, and to believe takes trust. When we trust God with our lives, we will need to be patient to wait upon Him for all things we ask for in prayer. We will need to accept His answer even if it is not what we want. The situation Ruth's in right now is waiting upon the Lord for the answer that is best for her life, not the answer she wants. We have all been in these situations and even if we have failed in the past, we can learn from our mistakes and do better in the future by trusting in the Lord and allowing Him to guide our path through patience and endurance.

Chapter 13: Redemption

Ruth 4:1-12

₁Now Boaz went up to the gate and sat down there; and behold, the near kinsman of whom Boaz had spoken came by. So Boaz said, "Come aside, friend, sit down here." So he came aside and sat down. ₂And he took ten men of the elders of the city, and said, "Sit down here." So they sat down. ₃Then he said to the near kinsman, "Naomi, who has come back from the country of Moab, sold the piece of land which belonged to our brother Elimelech. ₄And I thought to inform you, saying, 'Buy it back in the presence of the inhabitants and the elders of my people. If you will redeem it, redeem it; but if you will not redeem it, then tell me, that I may know; for there is no one but you to redeem it, and I am next after you.'" And he said, "I will redeem it." ₅Then Boaz said, "On the day you buy the field from the hand of Naomi, you must also buy it from Ruth the Moabitess, the wife of the dead, to raise up the name of the dead on his inheritance." ₆And the near kinsman said, "I cannot redeem it for myself, lest I ruin my own inheritance. You redeem my right of redemption for yourself, for I cannot redeem it." ₇Now this was the custom in former times in Israel concerning redeeming the exchanging, to confirm anything; one man took off his sandal and gave it to the other, and this was an attestation in Israel. ₈Therefore the near kinsman said to Boaz, "Buy it for yourself." So he took off his sandal. ₉And Boaz said to the elders and to all the people, "You are witnesses this day that I have bought all that was Elimelech's, and all that was Chilion's and Mahlon's, from the hand of Naomi. ₁₀Moreover, Ruth the Moabitess, the wife of Mahlon, I have acquired as my wife, to raise up the name of the dead on his inheritance, that the name of the dead may not be cut off from among his brethren and from the gate of his place. You are witnesses this day." ₁₁And all the people who were at the gate, and the elders, said, "We are witnesses. The Lord make the woman who is coming to your house like Rachel and Leah, the two who built the house of Israel; and may you prosper in Ephrathah and be famous in Bethlehem. ₁₂May your house be like the house of Perez, whom Tamar bore to Judah, because of the offspring which the Lord will give you from this young woman."

Redemption came to Ruth through the custom of leviratic marriage. The term is a derivative of the Latin word levir, meaning "husband's brother". The marriage specified that the nearest relative of a childless, deceased brother should marry his widow in order to carry on the family name. Such marriages were considered an act of love rather than a strictly enforced law. Deuteronomy 25:5-10 explained what the widow must do if a brother refused to perform the duty for her. She was to remove his sandal, in the presence of the elders, and spit in his face at the city gate. However, in this case, Boaz went to the city gate and called the elders in Ruth's place. He sought out the near kinsman and explained his responsibility to Naomi and Ruth. Boaz let him know right up front that if he was not willing to perform the duty that he would willingly take his place. Ruth would not be sent to spit in his face as was custom in Israel. When Ruth came to Boaz on the threshing floor, he knew that he was not next in line for her hand, and because of the way he handled the situation we can conclude that Boaz truly wanted to redeem her. She was young and he probably thought that she would rather have a younger man, but when she came to him, he was excited to see the matter through before the day ended.

Redemption is the repurchase of captured goods or prisoners; the act of procuring the deliverance of persons or things from the possession and power of captors by the payment of an equivalent; ransom. (Webster's Dictionary) Redemption laws were set by the Lord in Leviticus 25:23-30 for property that was sold. *"And in all the land of your possession you shall grant redemption of the land. If one of your brethren becomes poor, and has sold some of his possession, and if his kinsman redeemer comes to redeem it, then he may redeem what his brother sold."* verses 24-25. Redemption for Naomi meant that she could return to her possessions, redemption for Ruth meant that she was brought into the bloodline of the family. She was no longer a foreigner, destitute, and poor. She now had a place to belong, people to call family, and a heritage to give.

Boaz was to Ruth a redeemer as Jesus is to us a redeemer today, which is the purchase of God's favor by the death and sufferings of Christ; the ransom or deliverance of sinners from the bondage of sin and the penalties of God's violated law by the atonement of Christ. (Webster's Dictionary) Just as Ruth needed a redeemer to be in the Israelite family, we need a redeemer to come into the family of God. The redeemer God set in place was His Son, Jesus. *"In Him* (Christ) *we have redemption through his blood, the forgiveness of sins, according to the riches of His grace"* Ephesians 1:7 Grace is the free unmerited love and favor of God, the spring and source of all the benefits men receive from Him. (Webster's Dictionary) We can do nothing to earn redemption, *"but God demonstrates His own love toward us, in that while we were still sinners, Christ died for us"* Romans 5:8. Jesus was the ransom that paid our debt of sin and we are no longer foreigners. *"Now therefore, you are no longer strangers and foreigners, but fellow citizens with the saints and members of the household of God"* Ephesians 2:2:19.

Read Romans 3:22-26 and answer the questions below.

1. What is the righteousness of God? _____
_____

2. What does verse 23 say? _____
_____

3. What are we justified "by"? _____
_____

4. What are we justified "through"? _____
_____

5. Who did God set forth Jesus to be? _____
_____

6. What did God demonstrate? _____
_____

7. Who is He the just and the justifier of? _____
_____

"Therefore, having been justified by faith, we have peace with God through our Lord Jesus Christ, through whom also we have access by faith into this grace in which we stand, and rejoice in hope of the glory of God" Romans 5:1-2. The near kinsman told Boaz, *"I cannot redeem it for myself, lest I ruin my own inheritance. You redeem my right of redemption for yourself, for I cannot redeem it"* Ruth 4:6. The cost was too great a price to pay so he turned over his right to Boaz. Redemption was a gift to Ruth, but it cost Boaz a price. Our redemption is a gift to us but it cost Jesus His life. *"For the wages of sin is death, but the gift of God is eternal life in Christ Jesus our Lord"* Romans 6:23. Boaz willingly paid the price to have a relationship with Ruth, and Jesus willingly paid the price to have a relationship with us. Jesus paid a high price for our redemption so we could have a relationship with Him. So, let's rethink our relationship today and ask ourselves:

1. How much do I value the price Jesus paid for my redemption? _____

2. How much time do I spend in prayer? _____

_____

3. How much time do I spend in Bible study? _____

_____

Prayer and Bible study is your fellowship time with God. The Bible is God's Word and God's Word is Jesus. *"And the Word became flesh and dwelt among us, and we beheld His glory, the glory of the only begotten of the Father, full of grace and truth"* John 1:14. When we read it, then we put Jesus in our heart. Knowing God's word strengthens our relationship with Him, just as knowing our spouse strengthens our marriage. When we spend time talking with our spouse we build a bond that can't be broken. When we pray, we are spending time talking to God. Jesus instructed us to pray to the Father. *"In this manner, therefore, pray: Our Father in heaven, hallowed be Your name"* Matthew 6:9. Our prayer time with God is valuable to our relationship with Him. If we never talk to Him, it is doubtful that our relationship is strong or built at all. Just as our marriage would not be strong if we never talked or spent time together, the same is true in our relationship with God.

Recently I heard a story of a woman trying to witness Christ to someone. In her desperate plea for them to receive Jesus, she used the theory of Pascal's Wager, which is an argument in apologetic philosophy devised by Blaise Pascal. He says that humans bet their lives that either God exists, or that He doesn't. "Given the possibility that God actually does exist and assuming the infinite gain or loss associated with belief in God or with unbelief, a rational person should live as though God exists and seek to believe in God. If God does not actually exist, such a person will have only a finite loss (some pleasures, luxury, etc.)." So, basically, it is better to believe in God and go to heaven than not believe in God and go to hell. The first problem with this theory is that it encourages good deeds, living right, having a good heart, and excludes Jesus and the relationship altogether. We cannot do enough good deeds or live perfect enough to get into heaven. We are born with a sin nature because of Adam, and redemption for sin comes only through Jesus. *"For as in Adam all die, even so in Christ all shall be made alive"* 1 Corinthians 15:22. *"For by grace you have been saved through faith, and that not of yourselves; it is the gift of God, not of works, lest anyone should boast"* Ephesians 2:8-9.

The second problem with this theory is the existence of God. The Christian doesn't question whether God exists because we know Him in a relationship through Jesus. If we want others to receive Jesus then we must share Jesus, share the Gospel, and share our testimony with them. We need to love them with God's love and let them be drawn by that love which was demonstrated on the cross. We need to give to them as Jesus gave to us, and that is forgiveness, compassion, and love. We should want them to have what Jesus gave us, and that is eternal life. Heaven is merely the destination for us but our desire is for intimacy in a relationship with the Lord. When we are honest about our relationship and transparent about our testimony, we are more likely to encourage people to know the Lord, rather than condemn them to run from Him. This woman has a good heart and wants this other person to know Jesus, but in her ignorance, she led them away from a relationship and assurance of eternal life to good deeds and uncertainty.

Assurance comes to us in a relationship with God and it has been paid for by the cross of Christ Jesus, but are we neglecting it today? Have you received God's grace in vain? Do you go to church out of duty rather than out the love to hear His word and grow closer to Him? Do you claim Christianity as a title for the good deeds you do with a good heart? Do you question God's existence and try to live a good life just in case He is real? We should look deep in our heart for the answer to these questions. *"We then, as workers together with Him also plead with you not to receive the grace of God in vain. For He says: In an acceptable time I have heard you, and in the day of salvation I have helped you. Behold, now is the accepted time; behold, now is the day of salvation"* 2 Cor. 6:1-2. Salvation is the redemption of man from the bondage of sin and liability to eternal death, and the conferring on him everlasting happiness. This great salvation begins the moment we receive Jesus as our redeemer, and His blood covers our sin debt. We then receive eternal life instead of eternal death.

Read 1 John 5:6-13 and answer the questions below.

1. What does verse 6 say about Jesus? _____

_____

_____

2. What does it say about the Spirit? _____

_____

_____

3. What does verse 7 say? _____

_____

_____

4. What is the witness of God? _____

_____

_____

5. What does verse 10 say about those who believe? _____

_____

_____

6. What is the testimony? _____

_____

_____

7. What does it say about those who have the Son? _____

_____

_____

8. Why are these things written? _____

_____

_____

To believe on the name of the Son of God means that we trust that we can stand, rest, and reside in confidence with Him. *"Now this is the confidence that we have in Him, that if we ask anything according to His will, He hears us. And if we know that He hears us, whatever we ask, we know that we have the petitions that we have asked of Him"* 1 John 5:14-15. This confidence grows as we fellowship with Him in our relationship. Boaz and Ruth built a relationship of love and our relationship with God is built on love. Boaz redeemed Ruth because of love; Jesus redeemed us because of love. *"In this the love of God was manifested toward us, that God has sent His only begotten Son into the world, that we might live through Him"* 1 John 4:9. Let's examine our relationship today. Have we been redeemed by the blood of the Lamb? If so, let's love Him as He has loved us.

Chapter 14: Restoration

Ruth 4:13-22

13So Boaz took Ruth and she became his wife; and when he went in to her, the Lord gave her conception, and she bore a son. 14Then the women said to Naomi, "Blessed be the Lord, who has not left you this day without a near kinsman; and may his name be famous in Israel!' 15And may he be to you a restorer of life and a nourisher of your old age; for your daughter-inlaw, who loves you, who is better to you than seven sons, has borne him." 16Then Naomi took the child and laid him on her bosom, and became a nurse to him. 17Also the neighbor women gave him a name, saying, "There is a son born to Naomi." And they called his name Obed. He is the father of Jesse, the father of David. 18Now this is the genealogy of Perez: Perez begot Hezron; 19Hezron begot Ram, and Ram begot Amminadab; 20Amminadab begot Nahshon, and Nahshon begot Salmon; 21Salmon begot Boaz, and Boaz begot Obed; 22Obed begot Jesse, and Jesse begot David.

Restoration came once redemption was received. Restoration is the act of replacing to a former state; renewal; revival; re-establishment; recovery (Webster's Dictionary) and can be accounted to many different situations. However, it all has to do with gaining something back that has been lost, broken, destroyed, or taken. Naomi received restoration through Ruth's love and the sacrifice of Boaz. When Naomi came back to Bethlehem, she had nothing left. She lost her husband and both sons; she had no means of support, no lineage, and no inheritance. The only thing left in her life was the love of a daughter-in-law, which was the catalyst that brought restoration to her life. The neighbor women testified that Ruth was better to Naomi than seven sons would be, but during Naomi's "pity party," all she could see was what she had lost. She didn't recognize what she had standing right beside her in Ruth.

Sometimes we don't even realize what God has given us because all we can see is what we don't have. Ruth looked past Naomi's struggle and just loved her. We can play a role in the lives of people by loving them. Many times, we judge people in the middle of their trial instead of praying for them and loving them. Maybe that would be the catalyst to bring them to redemption and restoration, which is Jesus. Restoration is available to all of us, whether it is restoring the joy of our salvation or restoring us into a relationship with God that was taken when Adam sinned. Mostly anything we can think of can be restored if we will receive it. Our health can be restored by receiving prayer, medicine, or advice. Sometimes we just want the sickness to go away without doing anything. Our joy can be restored by receiving good news, forgiveness, or encouragement. Sometimes we find ourselves so unhappy we become depressed and we don't receive the goodness that could restore our joy.

Our relationships can be restored by receiving forgiveness, compassion, or acceptance. Sometimes we can get so hurt by someone that we harden our hearts against receiving anything from them or giving anything to them. These are only a few examples of the things that God can restore in our lives. There is also peace from chaos, laughter from mourning, clarity from confusion, light from darkness, and the list goes on. We can't have peace in chaos so we have to let go of the chaos to receive the peace. Jesus said, *"Nor do people put new wine into old wineskins, or else the wineskins break, the wine is spilled, and the wineskins are ruined. But they put new wine into new wineskins, and both are preserved"* Matthew 9:17. The "new" is available to us, but it is up to us to receive it. The disciples questioned Jesus while on the mount of transfiguration about Elijah coming before Jesus. *"Then Jesus answered and said to them, Elijah truly is coming first and will restore all things. But I say to you that Elijah has come already, and they did not know him but did to him whatever they wished. Likewise the Son of Man is also about to suffer at their hands"* Matthew 17:11-12. Restoration was available but they didn't receive it because they did what they wished.

If we want restoration, we have to let go of the old to receive the new. "Let Go and Let God!" I hear this saying a lot, but when I ask "how", the answer is always; "You just give it to God and let Him handle it." Really, this isn't an answer for "how", but merely a definition of the saying itself. So I will not be telling you to "let go and let God." I want to give you the tools you need to make a real difference in your life. So, the first thing we need to find out is what is old? Then, we need to find out how to let go of it. Since this varies from person to person, there is no specific answer; "how to let go" for one person may be repentance, but for another it may be acceptance, "what is old" for one person may be sinful living but for another it may be unhappiness. These things also vary from time to time; dealing with different "how's" and "what's" throughout our lifetime. However, they do work hand in hand, whatever things we need to let go of will determine the answer to how we do it.

Example 1: the old of sinful living is let go through repentance of sins and receiving Jesus as Lord and Savior by faith.

Example 2: the old of gossip is let go through repentance to God and discipline yourself to say nothing to others only to pray for those you used to gossip about.

Example 3: the old of pride is let go through repentance to God and humility to say you're sorry and admit you were wrong.

We deal with many things, but one thing we have to remember as Christians is that we are also human. As human beings we will make mistakes and lose heart, we will get prideful and gossip, we are not perfect, but we should desire to be. In that desire, we will find the courage to repent, forgive, and accept. We will find the courage to discipline our lives to be pleasing unto God. The key is to stay sensitive to God and apply His word to our lives. So, whatever is in front of us to let go of, God's word is where we will find the answer for "how to let go." When we read His word, attend church, and hear the message, God will quicken our heart to the old things we need to change so we can be more Christ-like in our living. The process of letting go of "what is old" to apply God's word to our life is the process of dying to ourselves. When we receive what is new, we are coming alive in Christ, and opening the door for restoration.

I have already shared some about my journey in forgiveness, but I would like to share one more story that opened the door to restoration. My brother, Travis, and I use to talk on the phone every day about God, His word, and our dreams to follow Him. Over time, we both got busy, I had young children, and he was going back to college so we rarely talked. As God led me into the ministry for women, I wanted Travis to be proud of me but it didn't seem like he was. So, in my hurt and disappointment, I put up a wall to protect myself. This caused more and more distance between us. God laid it on my heart to ask Travis to forgive me, so I did. During our conversation, I found out that he just needed to be encouraged. He had a series of events happen in his life and had some struggles. We prayed, laughed, cried, and forgave each other. This not only restored our relationship, but also was the catalyst that restored Travis' joy, and his direction with God. I had been so focused on myself that I didn't see his need.

So many people are in need of restoration. They have lost all hope for their life and have given up on any good for themselves. Maybe a little encouragement, compassion, and acceptance would be the catalyst that would bring restoration to their lives. *"Brethren, if a man is overtaken in any trespass, you who are spiritual restore such one in a spirit of gentleness, considering yourself lest you also be tempted"* Galatians 6:1. Too often, when we see others overtaken in any trespass, we help destroy them with harshness and discouragement, instead of restoring them in love and gentleness. We have a responsibility as Christians to help restore others and we should do it the same way Ruth did, in a spirit of gentleness, from her heart in love. For Naomi, restoration was only a couple of seasons away. During that time, Ruth was humble and teachable, submissive and obedient. She worked hard and did according to all that was set before her to do. People are looking for hope in this perverted world that we live in. They need to be encouraged and selflessly loved but because they are not finding it, they are looking for comforts in what doesn't last. Some use alcohol, drugs, or sex and we find them all around us searching for their next fix of happiness. Others use shopping, food, or money and we find them all around us getting temporary comforts from possessions, eating, or prestige.

We can all probably take an inventory of friends and family to find someone that is in need of redemption and restoration; someone that we can encourage with hope and selflessly love to restoration. As Christians, we should want all men, women, and children to know Jesus Christ as Lord. We should have a desire for them to be restored in a relationship with God. God's restoration is the final recovery of all men from sin and alienation from God, to a state of happiness; universal salvation. (Webster's Dictionary) We can give all kinds of advice and try to fix their problems but Jesus is really the only remedy they need. Once a relationship is established with Him, then all restoration is available. Our love and encouragement should draw them to one thing, Jesus. Maybe we can look at our own heart today and find that we need God's redemption or that we are going through a season where we are in need of restoration. Redemption must come first before restoration can be fulfilled in our lives or in the lives of others. We can reject God's restoration, just as the men did in Matthew 17, by hanging on to what we think, want, or feel. But if we will repent and allow His healing to take place in our lives with patience, then God can restore all things in our life.

Read Ezekiel 33:1-20 and answer the questions below.

1. What is the job description of the watchman for the people? _____
_____

2. According to verses 1-6, why is it so important to listen to the watchman? _____
_____

3. In verse 7, who does God say Ezekiel is? _____

4. What is his job description as watchman for the people? _____
_____

5. What does the Lord desire that He would set a watchman in place? _____
_____

6. What do verses 12-13 say about righteousness? _____
_____

7. What do verses 14-16 say about wickedness? _____
_____

8. What does the Lord say in verse 17? _____
_____

9. What does He say in verse 18? _____
_____

10. What does He say in verse 19? _____
_____

11. How does God judge according to verse 20? _____
_____

12. How can we receive restoration according to these verses? _____
_____

The key to these verses is "turn from". When we turn from righteousness and turn to evil, our life will die in sin. We can turn from evil and turn to righteousness so that we can live! This is not a message of losing salvation every time we make a mistake; this is a message of "turning from" God to live in sin and "turning from" sin to live in God. As Christians, we will make mistakes; this is why repentance, which means turn from, is a lifestyle for us. *"Repent therefore and be converted, that your sins may be blotted out, so that times of refreshing may come from the presence of the Lord"* Acts 3:19. *"If we confess our sins, He is faithful and just to forgive us our sins, and to cleanse us from all unrighteousness"* 1 John 1:9. God wants to give us life, He does not desire that we should die, but wants us to live. He wants even more for us than we want for ourselves so He allows us to go through things to help us grow into His likeness. *"Knowing that tribulation works patience; and patience, character; and character, hope"* Romans 5:3b-4. These trials bring restoration to different areas of our lives.

Restoration is given when we choose to receive newness of life, but it doesn't come in our time or our own way, that part is up to God. Naomi's restoration was only a couple of harvests away. During this time, God may have been teaching her to forgive her husband, accept her life, and love Ruth as she loved her own children.

For us, restoration could be a couple of seasons away, it could be a couple of weeks, or years, but during that time, we need to allow God to teach us. Maybe we need to forgive or accept, maybe we need to let go of our old way of thinking and allow God's restoration to fill our lives so that we can be a dispenser of Him to others. Whether Ruth knew it or not, she was a dispenser of love to Naomi. She cared for her even when Naomi had nothing to give in return. Ruth was satisfied with the new life she was given by clinging to Naomi. She asked for nothing more in life than to have Naomi's God and people call her own. With that gratitude and appreciation, she dispensed love and respect. This is something we should think about in our own relationship with God. Evaluate your relationship: Take a moment to pray. Search your heart and then answer the questions below.

1. Am I satisfied with the new life that Jesus has given to me? _____

2. Is the sacrifice Jesus made on the cross enough to satisfy my life? _____

3. Is it enough just to be able to call Him my God? _____

4. If God didn't answer another prayer or give me another blessing, would I still want to be in a relationship with Him? _____

These are tough questions to answer. We have all probably been at a place in our life when we have asked, "Where are you God." Those are times when we start searching our heart to see if we have sinned. His word says that He will never leave us or forsake us, so let's do the same for Him. Let's love Him as He loves us. Ruth and Naomi built their relationship on love and respect which grew closer and stronger as time passed. Their love and devotion saw them through the toughest times and lead them to deliverance from the rough life they lived. However hard or easy these questions were to answer, we can use this Psalm as a prayer to help us each day to remember how much God cares for us, how much we can trust Him, and His promise of restoration for our life.

"The Lord is my shepherd, I shall not want. He maketh me to lie down in green pastures: He leadeth me beside still waters He restoreth my soul: He leadeth me in the paths of righteousness for His name's sake. Yea, though I walk through the valley of the shadow of death, I will fear no evil: For thou art with me; thy rod and thy staff they comfort me. Thou preparest a table before me in the presence of mine enemies: Thou anointest my head with oil; my cup runneth over. Surely goodness and mercy shall follow me all the days of my life: And I will dwell in the house of the Lord forever." Psalm 23 (KJV)

Chapter 15: Happily Ever After

All fairy tales end with "happily ever after" and it is available for all of us through Jesus. Ruth gave us an example of a journey from sinner to saint, from destitute to bountiful, and from tribulation to restoration. Her physical life had a spiritual application that gave her a happily ever after. Her life now benefits our life as we learn to apply the same spiritual applications to draw us closer to the Father. This should give us hope that no matter what we go through in this life, God has a plan that will make us better on the other side of the tribulation and destitution.

Ruth clung to Naomi saying, *"Entreat me not to leave you, or to turn back from following after you"* Ruth 1:16. When Naomi shared what the consequences were of clinging to her, Ruth didn't let fear get in the way. When Orpah returned, Ruth may have been tempted to follow and go back to her old life, but she persevered with determination. She didn't allow anything or anyone keep her from staying in her relationship with Naomi. This is the same attitude we should have when we come to Jesus. We should not allow anything or anyone to keep us from our relationship with Him.

It is apparent that Ruth and Naomi had a strong bond that held them together, a bond that had respect, love, and obedience. This kind of bond with the Lord is what gets us to our "happily ever after." If we don't build a bond in our relationship with the Lord, we will not be happy in our Christian life. Ruth's life ended with a "happily ever after" because she made a decision to call the one true God, her God and to come under the wing of His people. She didn't come into the relationship thinking that everything would be a bed of roses; she just wanted to be in the relationship. We have an idea of what Christianity is, but when it doesn't meet our expectations, and we find out that it is not easy, then we are likely to follow in Orpah's footsteps back to our old life.

When we come to Jesus with predetermined plans of what we want Him to do for us, we set ourselves up for failure. Christianity is not about what God can do for us, He already did everything possible to have a relationship with you, through His Son Jesus, and it is up to us to receive Him in a relationship of love. Being a Christian is not about fixing our finances, marriages, addictions, or messed up life. God can do all these things as we build our relationship with Him, but building our relationship is what being a Christian is about. God didn't send His Son to die so that we could live in sin, or claim Jesus because we go to church on Sunday. God didn't send His Son so that we can have a hefty wallet or prestige and fame. The reason God sent His Son to die for us was so that we could have a relationship with Him. This is why the relationship is so important, because it cost the life of His Son Jesus. God has given us simple instructions in His word for building our relationship.

Read 1 Peter 2:1-5 and answer the questions below.

1. What purpose is given for laying aside these things? _____
_____
_____

2. How do we grow? _____
_____
_____

3. What does verse 3 say? _____
_____
_____

4. What are we according to verse 4? _____
_____
_____

5. What does verse 5 say about us? _____
_____
_____

We are built up as we build our relationship with the Father through Jesus Christ. We are to lay aside some things and learn other things. We are to grow and desire the things of God. *"And whatever we ask we receive from Him, because we keep His commandments and do those things that are pleasing in His sight"* 1 John 3:22. *Jesus said unto him, "You shall love the Lord your God with all your heart, with all your soul, and with all your mind. This is the first and great commandment"* Matthew 22:37-38.

In any relationship, we have responsibilities to the person we are in the relationship with. In the relationship with Naomi, Ruth took on responsibilities that were not easy for her, but she did not slack in her faithfulness. Christians have responsibilities in their relationship with God. He gives us commands to obey, directions to follow, paths to walk, and statutes to uphold, but He also gives us the Holy Spirit to help us in these things each day. Ruth was given favor in the sight of Boaz, which helped her each day with her responsibilities. Being in a relationship with Naomi was not burdensome, just as our relationship with God is not burdensome, but in every relationship, there are responsibilities that cannot be ignored. If we ignore our responsibilities, then our relationship is selfish and empty, with no love for the other person, or no love for God. A relationship with Him is the most rewarding, fulfilling, joyful, life changing experience a person could ever hope for, but difficulties will arise, hardships will come, and our faithfulness to the relationship will help us overcome.

Read 1 Peter 4:1-11 and answer the question below.

1. What instructions are we given in verse 1? _____
_____
_____

2. How should the rest of our time here be spent? _____
_____
_____

3. According to verse 3, what have we spent our past following? _____
_____
_____

4. How does verse 4 help us understand what we will deal with in the world? _____
_____

5. What comfort of justice does verse 5 give us? _____
_____
_____

6. How should we live according to verse 6? _____
_____
_____

7. What warning are we given in verse 7? _____
_____
_____

8. What does verse 8 tell us to do? _____
_____
_____

9. What does verse 9 say to do? _____

_____

_____

10. What are we to do with our gift according to verse 10? _____

_____

_____

11. What does verse 11 say is the purpose for everything we do? _____

_____

There are some basic instructions in these verses that will help us understand that we were once sinners, following the will of our own flesh, but if we will arm ourselves with the same mind as Christ, we can live according to God. We don't have to avenge or defend ourselves; God will do that for us. We are to be serious, watchful, and prayerful about our relationship with God. We are to love others, be hospitable, and give of ourselves for the purpose that God can be glorified. We should treat our marriage the same way, giving to our spouse and putting them above ourselves.

There is hope for all of us to have a happily ever after even if we are already married or if we never get married, because the key is to allow God to be the focus. When He is the focus of our life then we allow Him to orchestrate wonderful things in it; starting with us. Ruth had a humble attitude, a teachable spirit, and an ability to submit. She was patient and obedient. She had integrity to follow through with her commitment. She learned to respect others and display compassion because she learned to love with God's love. Once God was allowed to make changes in her, then He could take this virtuous woman and orchestrate a wonderful happily ever after for her. And the same is true for us. We have to allow God to make changes in us, learn to love with God's love, and build the characteristics of Christ through a relationship. This will create a virtuous woman in us so that our life can be filled with a happily ever after to the end.

Because Ruth was willing to change and receive wise counsel, Naomi and Boaz also experienced a "happily ever after" in their life. What could we do in the lives of those around us if we would be virtuous in the sight of all the people in our town? I pray that through this study you have learned to be a virtuous woman and are experiencing a "happily ever after" as you allow God to orchestrate your life according to His will. I hope you have already begun to see changes in the lives of your family and friends that they may find a "happily ever after" in their life as well.

Take a moment to reflect on some of the key points that changed you through this study. Write them down, be honest, and share with others how God created you into a virtuous woman.

_____

_____

_____

_____

_____

Conclusion

Thank you so much for taking the time to study *A Virtuous Woman: The Fairytale Story*. I can look back over my life as a young girl and see how much I wanted the fairytale story, desiring to be loved. I can see how decisions that my parents made to divorce, move, and change jobs, set the stage for a course in my life. I remember how the Christians I met throughout my life set an example, whether good or bad. But, with all of the circumstances and situations that occurred, it came down to one thing; a choice. I had to make a choice. I could use these things as excuses for my life or I could be willing to change and allow God to have His way in my life.

When I came to know the Lord in January 2001, my marriage was falling apart for the second time. My husband and I had separated once, and I knew that if we separated again it would end in divorce. I began to look at how happy my husband was and how miserable I was and concluded that my unhappiness was because of something inside of me. My husband couldn't make me happy, work couldn't make me happy, my friends couldn't make me happy, and I cried out to Jesus to forgive me for my sins. I asked Jesus into my life and surrendered to whatever He commanded me to do.

Today, I am very happy inside, my husband and I didn't divorce, we have two wonderful children, and I love my life with the Lord. Now, I'm not going to tell you that our marriage has been perfect since, because it hasn't. What I will tell you is that I changed the way I handled our marriage, because God changed me on the inside. What I was looking for could only be found in a relationship with Jesus. He gives me hope, joy, peace, comfort, love, and a happiness that only comes from knowing Him. My happily ever after began the day I received Jesus Christ as my Lord and Savior. God has taken me on a journey of highs and lows, good times and bad, but through it all He has been my strength and He continues to restore my life as I continue to add virtue to my faith.

I encourage you to share your **testimony of salvation**, newborn babes in Christ are scared to share their faith, and that is exactly where Satan wants them to stay; scared. He will try to cause them to doubt their salvation and question their heart. The main reason for newborns to share their salvation is to strengthen their faith in Jesus. It is harder for doubt to creep in if assurance is present. The more we share the stronger we become. As we grow, we should be able to help lead others to Christ with our testimony. When we share what Jesus has done for us, we give them hope. We give them an invitation to receive Jesus into their life, and open the door for them to know the Father.

Our testimony is more than just our salvation, there are other testimonies that we can share about our journey with God. Share your **testimony of restoration**. Express how God has restored areas of your life. This will give people hope that God can restore their life also. Restoration can be in our relationship with God, our relationship with our spouse, children, or other family members; it can even be in our church family. Restoration can be in things such as joy, health, and years. Restoration is allowing God to heal whatever is diseased in our life.

It is also important to share your **testimony of trials and tribulations**. Tell others how you made it through to give them hope that they can make it too. It also helps you become stronger in that area of your life. The trials we go through is to build character and produce endurance so when we share that trial it becomes a **testimony of growth** and keeps us from reverting back.

Sharing your **testimony of repentance** with others is important to help them see that you are still human and they don't have to be perfect to be a Christian, but that repentance is a lifestyle of a Christian. This doesn't necessarily come with a trial, it could be something you said, something you did, or an attitude you had. Sharing this will also keep you humble and relying upon God. It will hold you accountable to growth in this area of your life. I hope my testimonies throughout this book have helped you understand how to share with others. I pray this study has helped you to become a virtuous woman, that your happily ever after is being orchestrated by God, and overflowing into the lives of others.

Written in Love,

Sharon Hoskins

www.ingramcontent.com/pod-product-compliance
Lightning Source LLC
Chambersburg PA
CBHW081538040426

42447CB00014B/3423

9 780990 824510